NO THANKS, I'M FULL

BREAKING THROUGH DYSFUNCTION AND FINDING UNCONDITIONAL LOVE ALONG THE WAY

BY DEBBIE PAYNE

 FriesenPress

One Printers Way
Altona, MB, R0G 0B0
Canada

www.friesenpress.com

ISBN
978-1-03-912670-1 (Hardcover)
978-1-03-912669-5 (Paperback)
978-1-03-912671-8 (eBook)

1. BIOGRAPHY & AUTOBIOGRAPHY, PERSONAL MEMOIRS

Distributed to the trade by The Ingram Book Company

TABLE OF CONTENTS

Acknowledgements...xi

Introduction: Shedding the Shame..xiii

Chapter 1: Fasten Your Seatbelts . . . It's Going to Be a Bumpy Ride!.. 15

Chapter 2: A Young Bride at Sixteen..29

Chapter 3: Turning Up the Heat with Matt..37

Chapter 4: The Wake-up Call...45

Chapter 5: New Beginnings, Age 30..49

Chapter 6: Bigger than Us..55

Chapter 7: Little Did I Know..73

Chapter 8: A Letter to Coco...77

Chapter 9: Gale and Butterflies...81

Chapter 10: Finding the Silver Lining..91

Chapter 11: Taking My Health for Granted..97

Chapter 12: Before the Last Petal Drops..121

Chapter 13: Thank God for Friends..129

Epilogue..135

This book is a memoir.

It reflects the author's present recollections of experiences over time.

While all the stories in this book are true,

some names and identifying details

have been changed to protect the privacy of the people involved.

To my son, Austin . . .
My love for you gave me strength I did not know I had.
You gave me courage to change and the determination
to build a better life for you and for me.

You are, and will always be, the best part of me.

In memory of my sister Gale . . .
I am donating a portion of the proceeds of my book to
Canadian Mental Health Association (CMHA).

ACKNOWLEDGEMENTS

I want to acknowledge my dear friend Cheryl McFarlane, who spent endless hours, alongside me at my kitchen table, transcribing my "first shitty draft" right up until the last version of my manuscript. Thank you for steering me away from my continuous use of the word "now." I couldn't imagine sharing my first journey of writing a book with anyone else. Thank you so much, from the bottom of my heart, for always being there and loving me unconditionally.

INTRODUCTION

Shedding the Shame

With dysfunction comes shame—a word so small but with so much weight. Depending on the environment you're born into, you become aware of its existence way before you are given a chance to grow into adulthood, way before you understand the damage it can do, not only to ourselves but others. We can get so comfortable with it, we unknowingly pass it on to others. Shame on you for not doing what I expect! Shame on you for feeling the way that you do! Shame on you for not being financially successful, emotionally stable, the perfect parent, or, better yet, the child that never disappointed! I could go on . . . but you get the drift.

As a child, I felt and witnessed shame all too often. This disruptive, unworthy feeling was with me every day. It would remain with me until my fifties. When you are brought up in a dysfunctional environment, shame becomes a big part of your DNA.

Our childhood circumstances need not dictate who we become as adults. For those of us that are born into dysfunction, there is a disadvantage right from the start. It's more challenging for us to see what a gift life is and all that it has to offer, as we were programmed from infancy to believe the limitations that were put on us. We were taught that we are not worthy of being happy.

Life's journey takes us all in different directions: some for better, some not so much. Without a solid foundation from the start, our decision making can, more often, mislead us into circumstances with devasting consequences. Nevertheless, I think, despite life's disappointments, heartbreaks, and losses, in the end, it's still worth giving it our all. Because the love, laughter, and connection we experience between us is an intoxicating gift and reminds us all why we are alive! We can either choose to grow and embrace life with all its imperfections or shut down and be disconnected.

No matter how long or short our journey is, we owe it to the world, and to ourselves, to be our "very best"—whatever that "best" may be. Somehow making a difference in our world, whether that means finding a cure for cancer, making the best cheeseburger ever or raising your child to believe in themself and to have love and compassion for others. When we finally realize we are all connected, it opens so much more of life to us.

Unconditional love should be offered without limitations or conditions. We can experience this amazing and wonderful gift from our human counterparts, as well as from other species with whom we share this big, beautiful world. As humans, whether we admit it or not, we all crave this kind of love. It feeds our soul and makes us feel good about ourselves. Hell, even the fish swimming aimlessly in his bowl could be sending you love vibes, looking for it in return.

Through my own spiritual awareness, I have chosen to live my life—with all its blessings and hardships—to the fullest, trying to understand the lessons given and trust the process. I am grateful I have had people along my life's journey that loved me unconditionally. Some people helped show me my self-worth and added happiness to my existence while others took it away. To learn how to unconditionally love yourself first is the most valuable and most important gift you can give yourself. Life is a risk from the time you wake up until you take your last breath. I say make the ride count and let them know you were here!

CHAPTER I

Fasten Your Seatbelts . . . It's Going to Be a Bumpy Ride!

How excited I was for our weekly grocery store shopping trip. For all of us kids, this was something we all looked forward to as we knew a special treat was possible. My mother didn't drive, so all of us piled in the brown panelled station wagon, and off we went with my father driving. Returning home, a dozen donuts sitting in the back seat, I already had mine picked out. As my parents got out of the car, I was not prepared for what I was about to see. Unfortunately, this memory would stay etched in my mind to this very day.

I could tell my parents were arguing about something as they walked toward our home. My mother—with a huge belly, ready to give birth to my sister—crossed over our front lawn as she headed to the front door. My father followed behind her and, out of nowhere it seemed, pushed her to the ground. My first instinct was to run and help my mom, as most children would do under these circumstances. As I ran to help her, my father, ever so calmly, continued walking to the front door, never glancing back, as if it had never happened. My mother, now with tears in her eyes, slowly raised herself up from the ground. Seeing this, I started crying, especially when I saw the state of her bare knees, which were all scratched up and bleeding from falling on several stones. Without a word, she grabbed my hand and we went inside. This was my first memory of violence toward my mother.

When I was five years old, we had just moved to a home located right beside the school I would be attending. I thought this was so cool, to be living beside a huge playground. My younger sister, Lisa, and Justin, my older brother by four years, would also be attending that school, while our older sister, Gale, was in high school.

On my first day as a kindergartener, I remember how much I loved the pink plastic playhouse located in our classroom. It was big enough just for us kids to go in. The table and chairs that were inside had been set up and ready to serve imaginary tea with a child's tea set. There was a pretend pink plastic phone on one of the walls and a small stool for your favourite doll or stuffed animal to sit on. Oh, how I loved that house! When recess would come, I would ask to stay in the classroom just so I could explore and play in it all by myself. It became my happy place where I felt a sense of calmness and joy. There were no sounds of fighting here!

By age seven, I was beginning to realize how much time my mother spent sleeping in her bedroom, but it wouldn't be until my teenaged years that I discovered that she suffered from major depression. When my mother was awake, life was stressful for us all, as she was unhappy most of the time. Our home seemed always in a state of disarray. Piles of different-coloured clothing lay on the cement basement floor by the laundry machine, ready to be washed but seldom actually put in the washer. I remember once, all of us being asked, "Who threw these dirty clothes in the wrong colour pile?" None of us understood why this was so important or why this made her so mad. When we all said we didn't know, her temper flared up, yet again. My sister Gale being out, the three of us were forced to pull down our pants and were beaten on our behinds with a long red wooden stick. Sometimes, we were beaten so badly, we had deep welts, which made it painful to sit down. This stick belonged, at one time, to a children's broom and, now missing the top part, had become a weapon of violence.

Although it would seem to the outside world that we were just an every-day, average family, behind closed doors a different truth played out. We were children trying to cope with parents who were highly dysfunctional, each in their own way.

My brother, who had wished I was born a boy, didn't let my gender stop him from having a playmate. We sometimes played with army men—small plastic figures, some with guns in hand—and I, somehow, always seemed to lose the war. I didn't mind, though; I looked up to my brother and would have done just about anything to get his approval.

There, however, was a dark side to my brother, which would come out, periodically, from nowhere. We lived in a two-story home with steep, long stairs that lead up to the second floor. Once while my parents were out, my brother stood at the end of this staircase and dared me to jump from the top, saying he would catch me. Believing him, I jumped off the top landing, but as I did, he quickly moved away from the bottom and I tumbled down the stairs. I cried not only from the cuts and bruises, but from disbelief of what had just happened—that the brother whom I looked up could have done such a thing! Luckily, I had no broken bones, and after my parents returned home and discovered what had happened, they grounded him for a very long time.

Another incident such as this was one that left a physical scar. The three of us were with our mother as she grocery shopped. We were given pennies to go and get some gumballs from the machines at the entrance. Our favourite part of going! So, my younger sister, Lisa, went first, getting her favourite colour of gum. David got his, and then it was my turn. David placed the penny in the slot and told me to put my finger in the hole to retrieve it. As I did, he turned the handle. I cut into the tip of my finger. I screamed so loud, I think the whole store heard me! As I pulled my finger out, the blood gushed out everywhere. I had never seen so much blood before! All these years later, I still have the scar on the top of my finger from this memory and realize that any demons my brother was dealing with then were surely amplified by the toxic environment we were living in.

Around this time, my world was about to come to a sudden halt. One day, after school, while walking toward my home, I saw an ambulance in my driveway. As I got closer, I realized my mother was on the stretcher being put into the ambulance. I felt overwhelming fear and confusion as to what had happened to her. After the ambulance pulled away, I entered the house. With tears in my eyes, I looked to my father for an explanation. He said she was sick and needed to go to the hospital but would be back soon. Feeling scared, I wondered if I would ever see her again. When my mother returned, days later, I felt it was like looking at a stranger. She was devoid of emotion and eerily quiet. Watching her like this brought about a very uncomfortable feeling in me, as, usually, it was the opposite when she was awake. Normally, my mother would be upset or angry at something. It didn't take long, though, until her familiar self reappeared with all its sadness and unhappiness.

Although my father never raised a hand against us kids, unfortunately, I witnessed several incidents that revealed his violent nature toward my mother. Eventually, this created an unsettling relationship in the years to come between my father and I, as it brought up my feelings of abandonment and disrespect. However, there were a few good memories, like going for ice cream with my father on a hot summer's day as a young child and having family barbeques when conditions were calm in the household.

My father came from a family of seven. My grandmother had red hair, and as far back as I can remember, it was always in pin curls. A gentle, unpretentious woman who made me feel at home when visiting, she always spoiled us the few times a year we visited her with many baked treats. My grandfather, on the other hand, was a bigger man than my father and was rough around the edges. There was no mistaking as to who was the boss in this household. He loved playing cards and slept by himself in one of the two bedrooms on the main floor (the larger bedroom of course), which was set up with a card table and chairs. During our big family gatherings, which consisted of my many cousins, aunts, and uncles, the men would retire there after our dinner to play cards as the women cleaned up and my cousins, my brother, sisters, and I would play together.

As I entered womanhood, I started having an uneasy feeling around my grandfather. On one occasion while visiting my grandparents' home, after my father's twin brother's funeral, I understood why I had these feelings. As my grandfather held his arm around me from one side, he proceeded to grab hold of one of my breasts. I immediately pulled away while he laughed, thinking it was funny! It was after this incident that I started realizing that not all is what it seems. Unfortunately, this would be my last memory of him before he died.

My father seemed to have a decent relationship with all his siblings. He had an older brother and a brother, as mentioned, that was his identical twin, named Lloyd. My father's name was Floyd, but believe me, they couldn't have been any more different! My father had always worked in the business world, wearing suits and ties, whereas Lloyd was quieter yet drove a Harley and ran with a whole different crowd than my father. His two older sisters couldn't have been more different from one another as well; however, they both made efforts in planning family get-togethers throughout the year, which I always looked forward to.

Unfortunately, when I was nine, my world was soon to become even more unstable. Although my mother had a hard time functioning with everyday life, she did not turn a blind eye to the fact that my father was engaging in pleasures that didn't involve her. Him staying out till early hours in the morning told her all she needed to know. After what I'm sure was years of unhappiness in her marriage, my mother somehow found the courage and strength to leave. Looking back, I realize even more, the courage it took her to leave my father, especially in the late sixties. Yet, at the time, it seemed out of nowhere that the three of us and our mother were sitting in a mover's truck, packed with the contents of our home. I hoped I would like this place called Chatham.

Gale, the oldest at seventeen, stayed in Sarnia, as a friend and her family took her under their wings. Thankfully for her, this was finally some loving support and stability! Up until now, Gale had endured the worst abuse of us all. You might ask why? Well, it was mere fate, as she was the first born and my mother did not want and was in no way ready to be a mother. Mother would remind us of this on a regular basis. I remember one such incident when Gale needed to get glasses, but she was not allowed to choose the ones she liked. This had to be my mother's choice. After arriving home, Gale expressed her dislike of the glasses, and so my mother, upset, grabbed them out of Gale's hand, threw them on the ground, and stomped on them, saying, "Now you don't have anything to complain about." I was shocked that my mother behaved in such a cruel manner toward Gale and I felt sorry for my sister.

Our new home in Chatham was in a smaller community, and we didn't know a soul. However, I did know that my mother's father lived only twenty minutes away from us, and I hoped that I would get to see him. The four of us settled into an average-looking fourplex, where three other families lived, and I later discovered that we were all families on welfare. At this time, I began noticing boys and experienced my first crush living here. His name was Tony, and he lived in the building as well, making it easy for us to hang out together. He had thick, curly brown hair and dark brown puppy-dog eyes. We were in the same class at school and decided, one time at recess, to explore kissing. After, I could hear whispers from some other kids that saw us, saying that we were "necking." I had no idea what that even meant, but I liked it!

We called this home for two years. It was here that I learned how to ride a bike, blow bubbles with my gum, and went tubing in the summer months on a nearby stream with my brother and sister. My mother had no knowledge of this—otherwise, she would have forbidden it! Not so surprising since my younger sister, Lisa, and I didn't know how to swim. This turned out to be an escape for us of all. We could pretend, for a little while, that our world was filled with adventure and no stress.

For reasons unknown to us kids, we were moving again, this time to a bigger city called Hamilton, which was where my father lived. I found this confusing. If my mother hated my father so much, why Hamilton? I had not seen him in two years. In all fairness to him, he did try to see us, but my mother would not have it. She often reminded us how she received no financial support from him and that we were lucky not to be sent to live in foster care. Although sometimes, I wondered if it would have been better.

My father, in the meantime, had remarried and was living with his new wife and her three sons on top of the mountain in Hamilton, so I wondered if we would be able to see him.

Living in this much bigger city was a lot busier and louder than what we were used to. Our home was now in a tall run-down apartment building in a dirty, scary neighbourhood. I had so much hope that things would get better, but things were about to get a lot worse!

We three kids and our mother were crammed into a tiny two-bedroom apartment on the eleventh floor. My brother had to sleep on the floor in his sleeping bag, while I shared a bedroom with my younger sister. My mother had her own room.

For some reason, we didn't have a couch to sit on. Why didn't we bring our couch? Most of the boxes we arrived with were scattered all over the apartment, and most never got unpacked. We only used the essentials. Our living conditions were now worse than ever, and I was more fearful every day that we would be taken away.

I found my mother was becoming worse. She was sleeping more; she was angry and stressed and rarely came out of her bedroom. It was not surprising that my brother wanted out of these living conditions. He knew that our father lived in this city, and he seized the opportunity to track him down. My father agreed to allow Justin to come and live with him and his new family. And just like that, at eleven years old, I was now the oldest child left behind.

I took on the responsibility of the weekly grocery shopping, my younger sister in tow to help carry the bags home. The grocery store was miles away, so we had to either take the bus or walk. My mother would write a list and give me the money, and when I returned home, she made sure that she was given back the exact change, to the penny.

Money was tight. By now, I knew what living on welfare meant. Somehow, though, from time to time, my mother always found money to send my sister and I to get her Kentucky Fried Chicken. I smelled the aroma all the way home, thinking maybe, this time, we would get to share in the treat. Unfortunately, she kept it all for herself. It did not seem to bother her in any way that she enjoyed this all on her own. Perhaps in her state of unhappiness and being heavily medicated, she felt justified. In sharing this memory, my heart goes out to this little girl and her sister, both unable to understand their mother's selfishness.

At this point, I was starting to question my mother's behaviour. Due to incidents like this, I began to feel an overwhelming need to have control. I would internally say to myself, One day, when I am making money, I will buy whatever food I want and eat as much as I want. I am surprised that later in life, I didn't acquire an eating disorder.

Although my mother rarely left the apartment, somehow, she managed to have an occasional date. One of these dates would take away what little was left of my innocence, making me aware that wolves can be disguised as men. My mother was in the bathroom, finishing getting ready, while her date, someone I had never seen before, was waiting in the living room. I didn't know where she met this man, but I remember feeling happy—seeing how excited she was to be going out, despite her inability to manage life. She was an intelligent woman with a witty sense of humour. I'm sure her blonde hair and striking blue eyes turned many heads when she did go out.

While I sat on my bed, reading, the bedroom door opened ever so slowly. There stood this stranger pretending to be interested in what I was doing. He asked, "What are you reading?" Before I knew it, he was sitting beside me on my bed and placed his arm around my shoulder. While showing him my book, his hand slowly moved under the opening of my top, down toward my barely-there breasts. At eleven, I had just started my journey into womanhood. I immediately stopped talking as I felt his hand cup one of my breasts. I am sure it was only seconds, but it felt like an eternity before he finished his assault. As he stood up to leave the scene of the crime, he uttered, "If you say anything, I will say you're lying." The predator that he was, he already knew I feared my mother from the look in my eyes and took advantage of this, as I'm sure he did with his other victims.

Although I had no realization of just exactly what happened, it left me feeling dirty and more confused and alone than ever. That night, as I lay in my bed to go to sleep, I kept telling myself, repeatedly, to forget this ever happened—once again using the coping mechanism that I had already mastered so well. I must forget if only to survive! I knew, somehow, this was more than I could handle. At this moment, I realized I had no control over anything, not even my own body.

For our first Christmas in our apartment, we had no tree, no presents, and no decorations. If my mother knew it was Christmas, she never let on. My uncle Charlie, who lived in Hamilton as well, my mother's brother, seemed to show up from time to time when we needed him the most and appeared that Christmas morning. He arrived, picking up my sister and I, while my mother lay in a drug-induced sleep in her bedroom. So, off we went with no idea where we would be spending Christmas.

Arriving at a stranger's home, where we would spend the day, I could feel a strong sense of pity in the air. Their whispers were a dead giveaway. Lisa and I each received a gift, one of those spare ones you have in the closet in case someone unexpected shows up, but deep inside, we knew that they weren't intended for either of us. Nevertheless, we were grateful for getting something. After dinner, which was a blur, we were returned to an environment that was all too familiar but were glad this day was over! As I lay in bed that evening, once again, I told myself, over and over, to forget that day, that year, ever existed.

I do believe it is our built-in coping mechanism that kicks in when continual trauma is just too much to handle. Mine was pushed down so deep that it would take me years before I was strong enough to be able to uncover it, deal with it, and come to terms with it all. Let's face it, most of us have some skeletons in our closet that sooner or later need to be dealt with—mine just happened to be a whole damn football team!

I was almost twelve years old when I was suddenly sent to live with my grandmother, my mother's mother, whom I barely knew. She also, lived in Hamilton. They hadn't spoken in years, and I wondered why they had reconnected. Perhaps, deep down inside, my mother knew her own health was declining and, as much as she had little to no relationship with her family, hoped they would turn out to be a safety net for us if needed.

My first night was spent sleeping on the plastic-covered couch in the living room. Waking up I could feel the thick plastic rubbing against my face. Where am I? Then my reality set in as I remembered where I was. It was a school day, which meant a long bus ride to another place I still hadn't had time to settle in to. With the few clothes I was sent over with, it didn't take long to pick out what I was going to wear. I hurriedly ate my oatmeal and said goodbye as I ran to catch the bus. After two weeks of feeling like an unwanted guest, I knew this was only going to be temporary since the spare bedroom remained empty. I needed a plan! Although I knew my mother's health was deteriorating, I wasn't prepared to be on my own, with my future living quarters questionable. I knew where my brother had contacted my father, who was a mortgage manager for Canada

Trust, so I tracked my father down, knowing he recently had taken Justin in to live with them. Maybe he would take me, too?

With some loose change, I headed to find a phonebooth and made the call. I'm sure I cried and sounded desperate, but to be honest, I can't remember. Arriving back at my grandmother's later that day, I shared what I had done. To say she was mad would be an understatement. She was furious! I couldn't understand why. I thought I was helping her by taking away an unwanted responsibility. As she made the call to my mother, I sat on the living room floor, tears running uncontrollably down my face. I was hurt and scared at how my mother would react, and I never got to speak to my mother or say goodbye. Little did I know that I would not see her again until I was nineteen.

Later, in my adulthood, I was surprised to learn that my grandmother had abandoned her four children, all at young ages, to go live a different life. My mother, being the oldest girl, took on most of the responsibility of caring for her younger siblings, on top of dealing with her dysfunctional father, who was now angry at being left alone with four children to raise. His abusive behaviour toward his children escalated, leaving scars, both physically and mentally. This, my friend, is how dysfunction and abuse are carried on from one generation to the next.

I moved in with my father, new stepmother, and her three sons, along with my older brother, who had his bedroom set up in the basement. My room was the dining room, which was located on the main floor. At first, I felt very welcomed. My stepmother, Lynn, offered occasionally to wash my hair in the kitchen sink and then would blow dry it for me. I enjoyed her home-cooked meals, as this was rare for me to experience. Friday night was movie night for us kids, with chips and pop provided. I felt secure in what appeared to be a stable environment. It did not take long, however, for the novelty of having a stepdaughter to wear off.

My first clue to the kind of dysfunction that lived here was about to unfold. One day, coming home from school, I opened the door to the house and could smell the delicious aroma of food. I was starving and couldn't wait to taste whatever this was. As I entered the kitchen, there was no evidence of any food at all. Apparently, my stepmother had prepared and served dinner to her sons before I returned home, even the dishes were done! The burners were taken off the stove, so I couldn't cook and, in plain view, was a jar of peanut butter and a loaf of bread left on the counter. Sadly, it was clear this would be my dinner. I could not understand how she could do something so cruel, but I later discovered that this would be a pattern whenever she fought with my father.

While living under the same roof with my father, Lynn would do all she could to make sure he had as little contact as possible with me or my brother. Exceptions were allowed on special occasions, such as birthdays or Christmas. To further limit my opportunity to see him, Lynn would be sure that their dinner was consumed in their bedroom, as he often came home late from work. I was old enough to realize that living in the same house with my father and seeing him so little was very unusual.

Looking back, I realize just how dysfunctional and insecure this woman must have been. How sad I feel to come to the realization that my father accepted and allowed this to happen. As difficult as it was living with my mother, at least I knew she loved me. My lack of self-worth and shame just kept deepening: my mother was unable to take care of me, my stepmother despised my presence in her home, and my father made no attempt to change these conditions.

When I was thirteen, I went through a phase of shoplifting with my best friend Kim. Well, okay, I became a thief! We increased our wardrobe that summer with the latest summer fashions—without being caught for months. It became just too easy, or so we thought! Unfortunately, we decided to up the game and thought it would be even better if one of us could go in the store, steal an item, and then return it for the money. Back then, sometimes, you could return an item without the receipt. I lost the straw draw, so I was the one entering a Woolco store with a wrinkled used bag in hand—talk about a dead give away. I needed go in, pick out the item to be stolen and returned, and then leave. I'm not sure why I chose, of all things, an electric shaving foam dispenser, but it was the perfect size for the bag I had. I slipped it into the bag and, nervously, walked around the store for what seemed like hours. Looking back, I might as well have entered the store with a sign saying,

"I'm about to steal something." Finally exiting the store, I realized I wasn't going far. Almost immediately, I felt the hand of undercover store security agent on my arm. Kim, oblivious to what was going on, waited patiently on a bench outside the store.

I had never been in an unmarked police car before, and I was scared of what was to come. When I arrived home, in the company of the officers, my father and stepmother were waiting around the table in the kitchen, a pile of clothing on the kitchen table. Every item I had ever stolen seemed to be displayed for all to see. I was horrified and did not understand why Lynn did this. Now what? You would think as a family, we would come together and deal with my sticky fingers. However, the next day, my father informed me as punishment, I would be shipped off for the summer to relatives that I barely knew living in different cities.

I guess on the bright side, I got to know some of my aunts and uncles a lot better. One of these aunts was a fabulous baker. I enjoyed overindulging in her many treats, and thanks to her, I arrived home ten pounds heavier—okay, maybe more like twenty. Another aunt and uncle's home I stayed at for a week was a whole different experience. They were very religious, structured, and extremely close to their five children. While staying at their horse ranch, where I fell in love with horses, we prayed a lot! The last two weeks, luckily, were with my sister Gale and her husband; their home was conveniently a five-minute walk from the beach and a place I could be free to just be me.

After summer, I was back home, preparing to enter Grade 9—high school finally! I was eager to experience what the life of a high schooler was all about. My "shoplifting friend" and I were now dating brothers, Jason and Brent. Within the first few months of dating, my friend and I decided we liked the other brother better, so we switched. Jason would turn out to be my first love. He was tall, handsome, and with the most beautiful aqua-blue eyes I'd ever seen. Being four years older, he had already done things that I hadn't yet, like owning and driving a motorcycle—and, of course, sex. I, on the other hand, hadn't yet gone all the way. Cliché, but I thought I had found my "knight in shining armour"!

After a year of Kim and Brent being together, they found out they were to become parents and were married at ages fifteen and sixteen. I, of course, was the maid of honour, and Jason was the best man. Within months, a beautiful baby girl arrived. Although they were still kids themselves, through lots of family support and love, they played house successfully for awhile. But, as we all know, the odds were against them and they parted two years later.

A year later, we would make the same commitment—no baby this time.

CHAPTER 2

A Young Bride at Sixteen

At fifteen, I found myself walking alone into a bridal shop to pick out my wedding dress. As this was my first time in a store like this, I was overwhelmed with all the beautiful gowns.

"Is someone meeting you here?" a voice asked out of nowhere. A petite woman, stylishly dressed, appeared in front of me.

"No, just me."

I instantly saw a look of surprise on her face. Taking me under her wing, this lovely lady helped me select my dress. Being on a tight budget, I found it challenging to find something I liked, but she helped me find a beautiful, traditional wedding dress with a veil. Trying it on, I immediately felt like a princess. Oh, such an incredible feeling, our first love!

The day arrived. It was your typical wedding back then in the late seventies: a rented hall filled with relatives, half of which I did not know, and friends who would enjoy a sit-down dinner, an open bar, and a band to follow. Our honeymoon was in Niagara Falls, but only for the weekend. I was still in Grade 11 and had to be back to school on Monday. Plus, we didn't have a lot of money. My teachers and fellow students all assumed I was pregnant, getting married so young, but I surprised them as I lost weight and radiated young love. I even joined the Drama Club, which I loved. Finally feeling good about myself and seeing what I could accomplish, I no longer lived with constant stress and, at last, felt wanted.

Our first year was filled with us trying to figure out what our roles were supposed to look like in marriage. I learned how to cook, do laundry, and even did a bit of sewing. I quickly learned that I "sucked" at them all. Jason was working full time at a gas station to provide the money we would need to live in our cozy, one-bedroom apartment. I was now in Grade 12 and was enjoying the spotlight, participating in theatre productions. We were quite liking our independence and freedom, enjoying this "honeymoon stage." Going into the second year, well, that was a whole different ballgame!

I started seeing signs of Jason's frustration and discontent. He was spending more time out with his friends and less with me. When expressing my feelings about how I felt, I quickly learned not to poke the beast! The first incident was a shove up against the wall, and I, of course, convinced myself he didn't mean to do it—he was just angry at the time. Later that day, Jason apologized, and because I so desperately wanted his love, I forgave him.

Within a few months, we moved from our cozy apartment to the top of a duplex. This represented a new, fresh start. For the first while, everything seemed new and alive again. We both loved being in this character home, filled with charm and with access to a backyard. The novelty soon wore off, however, and Jason could no longer ignore his own feelings of unhappiness.

Jason had a motorcycle and loved to ride. He also had a friend that shared his passion, and they frequently rode together. On this particular day, Jason informed me that he was going out, yet again, to ride.

I said, "What? Again?" I was feeling that old feeling of no control.

Jason ignored me while he got ready, which made me angrier. My feelings of loss of control and rejection took over. Over six feet tall, Jason towered over my five-foot-three-inch frame. Screaming at him, I followed him into the bathroom where he proceeded to bend over the sink, brushing his teeth. I felt ignored and dismissed, and in frustration, I started to punch his back. In what seemed like slow motion, he slowly rose, his hand clenched in a fist, and punched me in the nose. It hurt so badly, I thought my nose was broken. Like a helpless, scared animal, with my hands over my nose, I ran to our bedroom and curled up in a ball on our bed, sobbing and in shock. Jason said nothing and continued to get ready for his ride. The next noise I heard was him shutting the door behind him as he left. Laying there, it seemed, for hours, I was hoping this was just a bad dream and I was waiting to wake up. I finally removed my hands from my nose and saw the blood. At this moment, I decided I deserved better.

At seventeen, I was already sitting in a lawyer's office, seeking guidance on how to get a legal separation. I must admit, I will never forget the look on the lawyer's face. I doubt he'd ever had someone this young pursuing a legal separation. My naivety would come in handy here as, to me, this was just another blip on the radar. I had excepted my marriage was over. I made a promise to myself as a little girl that I would never let a man hit me, no matter what! Watching the physical abuse my mother endured was something I was never going to accept. Let my new journey begin!

I had already experienced so much at such a young age. My mother was dealing with her own trauma from a life filled with pain, loss, and abandonment and was not able to be there for herself, never mind for the children she should not have had. My father, as well, was unable to be there on an emotional or physical level, having suffered trauma in his own childhood. Unfortunately, their trauma would be passed down in ways that stayed with me for a good part of my life. I was now totally on my own, a young adult venturing into territory unknown. I was scared but excited at the same time. I was now able to make my own decisions and search for my own happiness, not depending on anyone else to provide this for me!

I knew working full time at Burger King wasn't going to cut it, now that I was on my own, so I put on my best digs and confidently walked into some higher-end restaurants in the city. I was eager to work in whatever position they would offer me.

Luckily, I was hired for a position as a hostess at a new, upcoming restaurant, which I gladly took. I got to dress nicely, smile often, and welcome patrons, and I got paid for it! After several months of doing this, I discovered I wasn't making enough money to live on, especially being a young woman who liked to shop.

A friend of mine had reached out and told me of a full-time position opening up in our mall for a sales position at the hottest trendy clothing store. Unfortunately, this would only last a year due inside politics, and I was fired! I was devastated and my self-esteem suffered terribly. With time off now, I headed to Sarnia for the summer to be with my sister Gale while I licked my wounds. Having a lot of time on my hands, I decided to track down my mother. I felt all grown up and was anxious and ready to see her after seven years. Fortunately, I knew the city she was living in and looked her up in the phonebook.

As I drove down the highway to the small city she lived in, I had butterflies in my stomach the whole time. Not knowing what to expect, seeing her after all these years, I was a young woman still yearning for her love and connection, as I did when I was a little girl.

I pulled up in front of an older apartment building, quickly realizing how run-down it was. Before I knocked on her door, I took a deep breath and hoped she would be as excited to see me as I was her. She was expecting me, but you would have never known it as she opened the door and simply said, "You're a lot heavier than I was at your age." As I entered into her apartment, I instantly noticed how little had changed. The few items that she did have were well worn and very tired looking. She was, as well. Unfortunately, the picture that I had in my head about this reunion and the reality was very different. Within minutes, she let me know she had very little food and no money. Overwhelmed with sadness, I offered to go to the corner store and get her what I could. The more we talked, the more I realized she was at an even darker place than I had once remembered. I wish I could say that this last memory of her was one filled with joy, love, or comfort, but the reality was that I felt no connection, no love. I felt like I was with a stranger. On the drive home, I had to come to the painful realization that this woman I had hoped would somehow get healthier did not have the support or strength to do so. I left her my address and phone number, but never heard from her.

As the summer drew to an end, I returned home to Hamilton, back to work at the restaurant. I was eager to learn and quickly understood how lucrative tip money could be. I quickly became used to making more money, working only twenty-four to thirty hours a week. I could afford a decent car now and the odd splurge in a high-quality garment. I was making new friends and loving my independence. Life was good!

While learning my new craft, I was taught by one of the best—shall we say a veteran at age twenty-eight—in the industry: Brian. He was flamboyantly gay and I loved hanging out with him. I found him so interesting, with his different points of view, and he always looked impeccable and smelled great! We both loved to dance and would go out on the weekend to our favourite disco, dancing the night away. We enjoyed shopping together, dining out, and, yes, talking about our boyfriends. This was my first experience loving a man and wanting nothing in return but friendship.

At twenty-one, I was invited to travel with my dear friend Brian and two of his gay friends. I thought, Now, this is going to be an adventure.

His friends had several time shares throughout Florida, which we would be visiting. This was my first time on a plane, and I was about to discover just how much I loved to travel. My favourite place was Key West. I loved the laid-back quality of life and the people—it was a very accepting place. At one of the many gay nightclubs, I was flattered to find an attractive young woman flirting across the bar with me. This was the first time that this had happened and it boosted my self-confidence: I was attractive, even to the same sex.

Throughout this trip, I also learned first-hand how two men together in a relationship behaved, and they had similar arguments and issues as a heterosexual couple would. An example of this was when we were driving down a highway in Florida, and they were arguing. With no warning, the car came to a sudden, full stop on the shoulder of the road. Francesco, the driver, quickly exited the car and ran toward the open field beside the highway. He was so upset with his partner that he removed his ring, a present from his lover, and threw it into the wide-open field. His partner looked horrified. After things had calmed down, we all walked through the field, trying to find the ring. However, it was like trying to find a needle in a haystack! I learned that day to respect that all relationships, regardless of their sexuality, had these moments of intense emotion!

Through all of our travels together, we grew closer and laughed lot.

I returned home to find that the restaurant where I worked would soon be closing its doors. With three years of waitressing experience, I went off to find my next job.

Guess who was coming to town and opening his first restaurant in Hamilton? Don Cherry. So, along with hundreds of other applicants, I applied. I remember feeling a sense of competition, and I liked it. Maybe this realization would impact my decision, a few years later, to become a realtor. I now knew that I liked change and challenges.

Meeting Don Cherry and not being a big sports fan, I was oblivious of the icon he had already become. He was just one of my bosses. The other silent partner ran the day-to-day operations of the restaurant. He was the opposite of Don Cherry, very quiet and reserved.

When first getting to know Don, he seemed to have a bit of a crusty exterior, but as I quickly learned, he had the personality and heart of someone you just couldn't help but like! He wasn't as boisterous in everyday life as people expected from seeing on TV. I remember one Sunday working, bored silly, when in walked Don Cherry in his tracksuit. At first, I barely recognized him. He said hi and proceeded to now walk behind the twenty-foot-long bar and started cleaning out the 100-gallon fish tank, which was in full view. I'm sure he could have afforded to hire someone to do this but must have found some joy and sense of accomplishment in doing this himself. Without him even realizing it, he taught me a lesson in humility as it was obviously not beneath him to do this time-consuming chore.

My position at Don Cherry's was a bartender, back when you did not need any specific certificate. I was trained on the job and loved the creativity of making good drinks. Oh, and the money was even better than waitressing!

Over the next six years, I learned more about people's psyche, probably better than any university course could have taught me.

One of the chefs at the restaurant was looking for a place to live, and I took her in as roommate. Boy, did she know how to cook! I thought, who knows, maybe I would learn a few cooking tips. I didn't like cleaning up a mess or the time involved in cooking, but at least I learned how to make an awesome omelet!

CHAPTER 3

Turning Up the Heat with Matt

One night, my roommate had invited me to go with her over night to visit a campground where friends were staying all weekend. By the time we got there, it was night fall and her friends were having a bonfire. Matt and Jason, friends of hers, were already well on their way from drinking all day. It didn't take me long to realize that this was a set up for me and Matt. Matt was nine years older; he had a medium muscular built and a sense of humour. His boyish looks could melt any woman's heart! He had a love of music, as did I, and liked to dance (totally oblivious, he was always out of rhythm!). I liked his confidence, though. There was an instant attraction for us both, and, yes, that night I threw caution to the wind and had the most intoxicating sex I had ever had, which would continue . . . and get better!

One weekend, we took off to Niagara Falls. We did a lot of the touristy stuff, like seeing the falls and going through the shops and wax museum. But I had no idea how one museum would create a memory that I would never forget!

Like most wax museums, it was dark and full of hallways with twists and turns. Halfway through, with no warning, Matt pushed me back into a nook off in one of these dark hallways. He passionately started kissing me while his hand went under my top, exploring my breasts. Being caught up in the heat of passion, I let him have total control. With both of us close to climaxing, the sound of faint voices getting closer only intensified our orgasms! Just in time, we got out of there before the dark shadows of strangers closed in on us.

After several months of dating, I was blindsided. After a long day at work, relaxing on the couch, I received a call from Matt. He was in jail, arrested for stealing a car! As upset as I was at first, I decided to go see him in jail. While visiting him over the next sixteen months, I learned about his whole other life. This was not his first time being charged, but it was his first conviction. Over this time, I saw how some people lived their whole lives in and out of the legal system. I felt for their loved ones, who had to cope with this lifestyle, especially the children. I understood just how strong we as humans desire to be loved no matter what the sacrifice—that was the power of love.

Sixteen months later, Matt was released. I believed, more than ever, that he loved me enough to change his evil ways. I was too young yet to understand that the odds of him changing were next to none, as this lifestyle was what he had grown up in and all that he knew. However, I believed that everyone deserves another chance.

A few months after his release, Matt wanted to go to Mexico. He had been working as a roofer and had saved some money so we could go on the trip. "Count me in!" I said. Acapulco, here we come!

We landed, flagged down a cab, and headed to destination unknown. We had no accommodations booked, so Matt asked the cab driver to take us to a hotel that he recommended till we got our bearings. We were dropped off in front of a sketchy-looking hotel. After checking in, it didn't take us long to discover the room desperately needed a makeover. We were in one of the least desirable locations in Acapulco, but we were tired, so we grabbed a bite to eat at a local restaurant a few doors down and called it a night. In the morning, we both agreed it was time to upgrade.

Our new accommodations were on the beach at an all-inclusive resort, where I got to see how the other half lived. People were waiting on us, bringing drinks, and we had several choices of restaurants that offered various selections of delicious foods. I was in heaven!

At this resort, Matt met Dan, who lived in Mexico six months of the year. He mentioned to Matt about another destination in Mexico called "Puerto Escondido," which was on the Pacific Coast and was not yet known to many tourists. He told us it was remote, picturesque, and inexpensive to stay. Since we were going to be staying in Mexico for the next four weeks, this sounded like the place to be.

The bus ride to Puerto Escondido would take six long hours, driving through the night. This vehicle, which carried us along with other locals, did not look particularly travel worthy. The back bumper looked like it was about to fall off. Since it was dark, as well, this night ride would prove to be the scariest bus ride I'd ever been on! The twists and turns of the roads and the condition of this bus made me wonder if we were even going to get there safely. After sleeping on and off for several hours, I opened my eyes, realizing the bus had, finally, come to a stop.

The sun was now shining, and I was thankful that we had finally arrived in one piece. Stepping out of the bus onto a dirt road, I looked around and realized this was a far cry from what I had just left. However, I was excited for a new adventure and to learn Spanish. Due to it being so remote, very little English was spoken here. There were only two hotels, one of which was for us normal folk and the other for people with money, and it had its own private pool. We were all set up to rent a one-room cement bungalow located somewhere on a hill off the beach. To get to this place, we had to walk down the beach for about a mile. With suitcases in hand and the sun beating down on us, my excitement was fading fast. Finally, we found this cement hut, and as we looked up at it, I thought, How the hell am I going to walk up this steep hill with a heavy suitcase in my hands? It held way more clothes than I actually needed. But where there's a will, there's a way! Now, finally at the top, the hut in view, I noticed right away there was no glass, or screens, in the window openings. I learned that this was typical of this area. It was small but, I guess, what more did we need?

As we entered this one-room villa, I saw a huge bug net over the bed. At first, I thought, Isn't that romantic! I didn't realize until later that it was to ward off flying bugs–big flying bugs. Thirsty from our climb, I looked for the fridge and realized there was none. I am an adventurous girl, but I do like a cold drink and my coffee in the morning.

Later that day, we grabbed dinner and drinks at the "affordable" hotel, geared for travellers on a budget, and indulged in fresh red snapper that had been caught by some local fishermen earlier in the day.

Upon returning to our cement quarters, I was tired. The last thing I remembered was saying goodnight to Matt under the not-so-romantic canopy of bug netting.

Hours later, I woke to find myself alone. To say I was scared is an understatement—the silence was deafening. Looking around, seeing the dark black night through the window openings in the cement walls, I envisioned that, at any moment, someone could come leaping through. My imagination was now on overdrive. I lay in bed, frozen with fear. This would prove to be one of the longest nights of my life!

When the morning sun finally arrived, I was grateful to be safe. Now, however, I was angry and started pacing the floor. Where the hell is he? Is he all right? Finally, Matt appeared, staggering through the doorway, obviously drunk.

"Where the hell did you go?" I shouted, "And what were you thinking, leaving me alone in such a remote area?"

Matt apologized but, in his state, went directly to the bed and passed out. I was so mad that I quickly packed my bag and stormed out, making my way down the challenging hill. I must admit it was way easier going down than up. With my adrenaline flowing, it didn't take me long to make the mile-long trek down the beach to the affordable hotel. I checked into the cheaper hotel that had no air conditioning, but I was thankful that the room offered some comforts of home, and I felt safe.

Later, while I was lying on the beach, Matt tracked me down and apologized. Seeing as I had little money, and Matt had the plane tickets to go home, I felt it was in my best interest to let this go for now. We spent the next several weeks at the hotel.

Because the locals ran what few hut-like restaurants were available there, I was forced to learn Spanish quickly, especially if I wanted to know what I was ordering. I loved being immersed in this language, culture, and the amazing food!

We met backpackers from all over the world and, after fishing one day, accompanied by local fishermen, we shared a pickerel dinner with some of them. With huge waves that day, let's just say I had my head bent over the sides of the boat most of the time. I chalked it up to having too many drinks the night before.

As the weeks passed, we were feeling more and more attached to this place! On Easter Sunday, we went to church. It was like nothing I had ever experienced. Even though I didn't understand most of what they were saying, I loved the sound of the language. I watched mothers freely breastfeed their babies while in church—something I had never witnessed before. This loving connection made me appreciate this place even more.

Our time in Mexico flew by, and our stay there soon came to an end. We said goodbye to the friendships that we made and the place that we both had fallen in love with. On our last night, we shared many laughs and drinks with our friends before our departure the next morning. By one o'clock, we headed back to our hotel, but as we were walking alone on the beach, we began to argue about something. Then, as if out of nowhere, three well-armed men in camouflage gear appeared, pointing their machine guns directly at us. They were forcefully yelling in Spanish, which stopped us in our tracks. With his charming personality, Matt immediately tried to assure them with hand gestures and a calm tone of voice that everything was fine. I was surprised I didn't pee myself, I was so scared. At this moment I thought, Oh my God, I am going to be killed and nobody knows where I am, other than somewhere in Mexico.

Thankfully, they lowered their guns and their aggression lessened. After accepting everything was now fine between us, they let us on our way. I felt like we were in a movie scene, and the director had just called "Cut!" I felt surreal. This was not the send off I had anticipated!

After five weeks of adventure, travelling in Mexico, it was time to face going home to look for a new job. One benefit of having restaurant experience, I never had a hard time finding work. I found work quickly and settled back into my reality.

I started noticing that I was feeling nauseous often and my breasts were tender. My periods had always been irregular, so I thought nothing out of the ordinary here. Realizing I had skipped a period, I thought I should take a pregnancy test. After the shock of seeing the "plus" sign wore off, I was excited with the results.

I realized I wanted this baby—I think to prove to myself that I could be the mother I never had. Matt, on the other hand, made it clear that, under no circumstances, did he want another child. He already had a seven-year-old son with his previous wife. He understood the scars his lifestyle choices were leaving on his son. However, there were moments that I witnessed this tough guy melt, especially when he was with his son, who was still so young and vulnerable.

So just like that it was over. I no longer had a life growing inside me. I knew that if I had this child, I would have no support of any kind, either financially or emotionally, from Matt. I wasn't sure who I hated more at this moment—him or myself. This by far was one of the most difficult decisions I have ever made! It would take years for me to forgive myself, but looking back, I realize that at such a young age, I had so much more to figure out about my own life and was not prepared to be the mother I wanted to be.

At this point in my life, I believed Matt was really the first man with whom I felt a deep connection, and I believed he needed me more than anyone he had before. I was hoping he would change to give himself and us a chance at a happy life. Boy, was I in for a reality check!

One weekend, while I was away visiting family and friends, Matt would become involved in a situation that would profoundly change the direction of his life and end the possibility of any future with me. With the help of two other convicts, one of whom was an escaped murderer, Matt, along with his bad-ass friends, planned the "perfect" heist: they were going to rob a Brinks truck.

Back now in my apartment, to which Matt had keys, they were dividing the money and cleaning up, so to speak. When I arrived home, hours earlier than expected, I heard voices as I unlocked the door to my apartment. Upon opening the door, I tried stepping in, but Matt was suddenly there, pushing me back out the door into the hallway. Pressing me against the wall, Matt, in my face, made it very clear that me being there "never happened" or my life would be in danger. Now, I was getting scared and wanted answers, but he ordered me to leave immediately for my own safety and to not return for several hours; then we could talk.

My gut told me that something bad had happened, but still feeling the need to believe in this relationship, I chose to wait for an explanation. Upon returning home, Matt said that these guys, not long out of jail, were just in need of a place to shower after helping him with a roofing job. They were his former cell mates, and he said that he just wanted to help them out with a job and a bit of cash. I wanted to believe him and chose to ignore my gut feeling that something more was going on. Again, Matt reminded me they were not to be messed with. He knew it was in my best interest not to have seen any of them, and, boy, he couldn't have been more right!

CHAPTER 4

The Wake-up Call

Early one spring morning, I woke up to a gun pointed at me before the sun had fully risen. Two detectives stood above my bed, their guns pointed at me and Matt. I don't think I ever screamed so loudly. Being that Matt and I were both naked in bed, they allowed us to get dressed while my apartment was being searched. Through this search, I kept thinking, Damn, I have some personal weed they'll come across. Little did I know how much more serious this situation would be–I had no idea how much more the heat was about to be turned up!

Matt and I were both put in handcuffs and escorted to the police station in separate cars. The whole time, I thought to myself, "This can't be really happening." On arrival, I was put in a small, enclosed cement room, with a chair to sit on, and the detectives told me they would be with me soon. I was scared shitless! I had no idea of the severity of this situation.

After waiting for what seemed like hours, the door finally opened and I had the company of the two detectives, one rather tall and stone faced, and the other shorter and on the plump side with a friendlier demeanour. I was questioned for hours, between bursts of uncontrollable tears streamed down my face. It never even donned on me to ask for a lawyer because I knew I had done nothing wrong, so when the detectives finally informed me why Matt and I were arrested, I was mortified! They made it clear that their impression of Matt and I was we were the next Bonnie and Clyde. I thought to myself, "I couldn't make this shit up."

I was truly shocked to find out that Matt had escalated from stealing cars to committing armed robbery on a Brinks truck. Oh, and let's not forget—with an escaped murderer! I know, I know, you're probably thinking, "Come on, you had no idea?" As hard as it may seem to believe, I did not. I knew he had stolen cars in the past, but I believed him when he said he wanted a better life.

Look backing at this younger version of myself, I feel sad that I had felt this desperate for love. If I never believed in guardian angels before, I sure did then. My love affair with Matt and his bad boy image came to a screeching halt! Without any doubt, I finally recognized just how close I had come to my life looking hugely different than what I had in mind. What a high price I would have paid in the name of love.

After the wake-up call, I wondered, "Where do I go from here? Who am I?" I was twenty-five, and my wake-up call, so to speak, made me realize just what an impact my choices were making on my life. Understanding just how close I came to going down a road of no return scared the hell out of me. I had to start to look at the choices I was making and why. One thing I knew for sure was that it was time for a new direction. Dating was no longer a priority. I decided to direct all my energy into who I wanted to become as an adult and how I could start loving myself.

One night, while out at the hottest disco nightclub in town with my bestie Lois, I met my new friend-to-be: Durago. He was fifteen years older than me, with thick jet-black hair and a moustache. He looked mysterious in an odd way and piqued my curiosity. His thick Eastern European accent made it hard for me to understand him at times, but, boy, he was a charmer! There was something that drew me to him. In conversation, I found out he had three daughters from his previous marriage and was a successful RE/MAX agent. I was touched by the way he talked about his daughters and how much he loved them.

Over the next several years, we become friends, and sometimes with "benefits." I learned exactly what a realtor did and, oh yes, the money you could make! I figured if this man from another country, whom I could barely understand at times, could be this successful, why not me?

While working as a bartender in the restaurant business, I proceeded to get my real estate licence, which, by the way, proved to be more challenging than I thought it would be. But, determined I was! Although it was discouraging failing the first and second classroom courses, I pulled up my big-girl boots and took them over again. Now finally passing these, I sailed through the third course, mostly due to the humorous and engaging instructor.

Over the next few years, I was determined to make real estate my full-time career. Filled with excitement and enthusiasm, I got hired right away at the bank Montreal Trust, which had started to dabble in real estate.

In the late eighties, there was little to no training available for new agents. On my first day, I was shown to my bare cubicle, where there was nothing more than a desk, a phone, and a phonebook. My task was to find possible clients. I was to make cold calls to strangers picked at random from the phonebook. After about two hours of countless rejections and hang ups, I felt totally depleted and discouraged. I broke down and cried and thought, "What have I gotten myself into?"

Thankfully, I was still working part time in the restaurant business. I still had bills to pay and needed to eat. In my first year, I only sold two homes. I felt like a failure, and my self-esteem hit rock bottom. However, on one of these real estate deals, I worked with a veteran RE/MAX agent named Frank. He was representing the sellers, and I the buyers. In those days, putting together a deal could take into the wee hours of the morning. Frank saw my determination in putting the deal together and recognized my potential. A few weeks later, he called and asked to meet me for a coffee. He piqued my curiosity as to what he wanted, so I agreed to meet him. He shared that he thought I had what it took to be successful and wanted me to meet with Ann, the RE/MAX broker/owner that he worked for. Little did he know, up until now, I had only sold two homes, but I thought if he believed in my ability, then what did I have to lose?

As I walked into the classy, beautifully decorated RE/MAX office, I felt very much out of my comfort zone. Why would they want to hire me? While I was waiting to meet the Ann in my $9.99 sweater, I felt like an imposter, that this was way out of my league. I saw other agents in their expensive business attire and thought, How am I going to pull this off? While waiting, I thought to myself, If I leave now, I don't have to prove anything to anybody.

Finally, in the meeting, Ann also saw my potential and gave me the opportunity that would change the direction of my career and my life. It turned out to be the best move I ever made! I was able to observe highly successful agents, performing at their professional best. Taking from this and developing my own style of doing business, I felt exhilarated and started believing in my own abilities to make this my full-time career.

Funny how life can bring you opportunities for growth when you least expect it and from people who were once strangers. With mentorship and support from Ann, I not only learned about real estate, but also learned to recognize and appreciate my own capabilities.

On a personal note, I now dated with no strings attached—a lot less messy! I still seemed to attract men with unhealthy issues, though. I didn't understand what a healthy, stable relationship looked like. I didn't even know if it was possible.

CHAPTER 5

New Beginnings, Age 30

Okay, time to grow up and be more responsible. After having a few successful years at RE/MAX in Hamilton, my father, who had opened his own brokerage in Sarnia, finally agreed to hire me on. When I first got my real estate licence, he made it clear that if I was going to make it, it was going to be on my own. As much as this hurt and with feelings of abandonment rising once again at the time, looking back, I realize he did me a favour. Thankfully, I believed in myself and became a successful realtor without him. I still so desperately wanted his approval, though, and yearned for his unconditional love. I now moved back to Sarnia in hopes of achieving this.

Being close to my sisters, Gale and Lisa, was exactly what I needed to create a closer family bond and new happy memories. I was excited for a fresh start and all the possibilities yet to come. My next journey in life would be facing realities about the people I loved and discovering all the layers of who they were, imperfections and all.

Being the risk taker I am, when the opportunity arose to buy my first home in this new city, I took it. I was temporarily renting a cute two-year-old bungalow, which had an in-law suite in the basement, from my father and his now third wife, Anna. Within three months of finally feeling a sense of family and less alone, I made the decision to stay in Sarnia and bought the bungalow from them. This gave me such a sense of stability and independence that I had never experienced before. Here, I would create a new feeling of security and comfort.

Over the next four years of working with my father, I spent more time with him than I had throughout my whole life. I enjoyed discovering things about my dad that I had never known before. Although he was still a workaholic, I recognized now there were worse traits to have. I loved our weekly breakfasts, where we would discuss everyday real estate dealings, future business to come, and so on. We now had a common bond. During each of these breakfast meetings, I chuckled inwardly, as every time, I could count on him spilling his food on his tie.

In getting to know his partner of several years, Anna, I soon realized who wore the pants. She had already established herself financially through her previous marriage to a successful builder and from drawing on her own business experience. My father and she were both workaholics, making this a very compatible relationship; however, I was disappointed in her lack of effort to form a close relationship with any of his three daughters, who were now all living in Sarnia. I always felt she was threatened by the possibility that he could form a close relationship with us. Years later, I would get confirmation of this. While my father and I walked down the street after hosting an open house in the same condominium complex, he told me he didn't want Anna to see me with him, as he was meeting up with her. When I asked why, he replied that she had some insecurities and he didn't want to upset her. It was at this moment that I understood he was as much to blame for the distance in our relationship as his partners.

Without really being aware, I started to disconnect with my father after having my son, Austin. As I began to better understand the role of a loving parent and how important their presence is, I could no longer turn a blind eye. However, this did not mean that I was ready or able to deal with this head on.

Before returning to my business months later, I did some soul searching. I realized that I no longer wanted to work for my father. As a young mother, I felt I needed to be working in a more supportive and professional environment. My father's idea of running a business was very different from mine. So, I let him know I would not be returning. I don't think he ever truly forgave me. I'm sure his ego was hurt more than anything. I understood that having a relationship with my father meant things needed to change in order for me to feel better about myself.

Now as a mother, I was working hard at becoming the parent I never had. Although recognizing it wasn't an easy job, it was my mission to protect my son from the type of trauma I had suffered.

Regarding the relationship I had with my father, I started taking off the bandage, so to speak, ever so slowly. In the past, I knew that having a relationship with him meant it would be on his terms. I was no longer willing to accept this. The cost was becoming too high. I wanted to take back control of my life and make decisions that were mentally healthier for me. Unfortunately, in order for this to happen, I needed to create more distance between him and I.

When I did spend time with him, it was an awakening experience, as I saw him in a very different light. Please don't misunderstand me; regardless of all his flaws and lack of connection, I still loved this man. Unfortunately, my father didn't want to change the ever-so-familiar dynamics of our relationship.

I needed to start looking closely at all of my relationships. Finally, I was beginning to understand the concept of setting boundaries, something I hadn't been taught as a child—and we all know how that turned out from the previous choices I made. My father would always be my father; however, I recognized now he would never be able to give me the healthy relationship that I so desperately craved. I came to understand he didn't have the ability or desire to redesign our relationship.

It still surprises me that regardless of the past mistakes he made as a father, his kids all still wanted a relationship with him. This, my friend, is the underlying bond that we all desire to have with our parents—and often at any cost!

Unfortunately, while going through this process of change, my father arrived home from his vacation in Mexico, not realizing he had suffered a heart attack. Unbeknownst to me and my siblings, he had felt unwell for several days. After which, he finally went to the doctor. He was sent home with no diagnosis, and he progressively got worse. For the life of me, I still wonder why anybody that knew of his failing health didn't insist on him going to the hospital. Perhaps someone tried, but I'll never know.

That following Saturday, I tried calling him several times with no answer and no return call. By Sunday, I was beginning to worry. I called my sister Lisa to see if she would go check on him. The next phone call I received I did not expect. My father had been transferred to a specialized hospital, an hour away, that dealt with heart attacks and strokes. Unfortunately, it took him several days to finally get the help he needed. He now knew he had suffered a heart attack and it had caused extensive damage to his heart, triggering several strokes.

Between all of Anna's five children, his children, and multiple grandchildren, I don't think the hospital was prepared for these many visitors. My father lay in the Critical Care Unit. As I walked in the room, I saw my sister Lisa sitting on one side of his bed and holding his hand. I was shocked to see how frail and helpless he looked. Several strokes left him unable to speak or move his left side. Although we had not seen eye to eye in the past few years, my heart broke seeing him in this condition. I walked to the other side of the bed and took hold of his hand while gently caressing the top of his head with my other hand. Tears streamed down my face as I told him I loved him. There were moments I felt his hand try to move away–or at least, this is what I thought–and it cut me to the core. I thought to myself, "Are you really going to spend our possible last moments together rejecting my love?" He would pass away, days later, in the middle of the night.

What a mess you left! As I processed my own grief, I came to learn that, months before his passing, my father had removed me as an executor of his will, leaving my brother and his twenty-one-year-old son, David, to the task. Coincidentally, David had moved from Hamilton to Sarnia only eighteen months prior, supposedly to help my father out with his business. This would include setting up appointments for showings, computer technology, paperwork, and, at times, driving my father to appointments, as his sight was diminishing in one eye. My understanding was that David had finished college and couldn't get a job in his field. So, this, I thought, was a way for him to make money while helping my dad out, but as I came to learn, it was for much more diabolical reasons. This would be a way for my brother to have influence over our father, even when he couldn't physically be there. David had become his father's eyes and ears. I did wonder why my brother was avoiding me during his visits over this time period—which, by the way, seemed much more often. Prior to this, he had welcomed the opportunity to stop by for dinner and a beer before his journey home. As my nephew lived with and worked for my father, he had begun to gain his trust. David came to discover how my relationship with my father was currently on the rocks, so to speak. I had shared some of my feelings about him with David once when I invited him over for dinner and a sleepover, having no idea how sharing this would be used against me!

I had learned a very valuable lesson: money, indeed, is the root of all evil. Regardless of sorrow and pain, when it comes to money, the true ugliness of people can emerge with all its glory, forcing us to see what relationships exist or don't exist and how people rationalize what is right and wrong when it's to their benefit. In a way, it was ironic that, as in his life, after his death, my father continued to destroy relationships that should have been so valued!

My brother, now having full control over the estate, sold off the ten homes my father owned. Not surprisingly, he used another realtor that worked for a different company than mine. As my father and I were well known in this small real estate community, this would only add salt to my opened wound. My brother's need to have all the money trumped the relationships with his sisters. How sad that he valued us so little!

Months later, we lost my sister Gale to a cancer that had returned for the third time. Overwhelmed by it all, I never fought to get my share of the inheritance, as I just didn't have the strength. I felt that, in a matter of a year, I had lost my father, my sister, and my brother. My sister Lisa was in good financial shape and decided, as well, not to pursue her share of the inheritance. To this day, my brother is the only person in my life that I have not yet been able to forgive. However, did I mention I do believe in karma?

Up until now, I haven't said a lot about my younger sister, Lisa, as our relationship, unfortunately, was on and off throughout the years.

When it was good, it was great! When she would cut me out of her life with no explanation—time and time again and sometimes for year—it just got too draining and I could no longer trust having a relationship with her, knowing this was a continual pattern. Early years, living in chaos and dysfunction, affected us all in different ways, and sometimes not all wounds could be easily healed.

Lisa and I did not speak for years, but I still had a relationship with her adult son. I'm sure this bothered her, and eventually, she found a way to end this relationship. During the past few years, I came to discover through my son that my mother had passed away. When I asked Austin, who told him, he replied that it was my nephew. I couldn't believe this was the way I found out. Lisa was the only one that knew of her whereabouts and chose not to disclose this to me. My mother had been gone for a few years, and my sister, who knew, chose not to tell me. Lisa's total lack of empathy and compassion in not telling me of my mother's death made me realize just how little she cared for me. I love her and wish her nothing but the best, but I have chosen to live the remainder of my years on this earth surrounded by people who love me and are able to be present fully—those with nothing to hide and no underlying resentment.

CHAPTER 6

Bigger than Us

For me, being a parent is learning the commitment, patience, and love it takes to help another human grow and find their wings to fly into their own heights of discovery, feel loved unconditionally and supported, and believe in their abilities.

I met Greg within months of moving to Sarnia. I was out with a friend one night at a bar, and we noticed one another from afar. He sent over a drink, which then sparked a thank-you from me, followed by flirtatious conversation. Greg was a charmer and had the looks to go with it. He had auburn curly hair and fair features, was sharply dressed, and stood tall with confidence. Before I left that night, I had given him my number.

He took several days to call, and when he did, we planned a date. The restaurant was one of the nicest in town, and as I sat down, I noticed a rose on my plate. How thoughtful! Okay, now you have my attention, I thought. He ordered a nice bottle of wine, and we talked easily, with lots of laughter, for hours. I was intrigued and wanted to know more. Over the next several months, I was hooked and fell love. Greg was very attentive and often surprised me by showing up with the most beautiful cards and flowers, and on top of that, he could cook. I thought I had finally hit the jackpot!

It was a natural progression that Greg would now move in with me. Living together, however, would show a different side of Greg that I hadn't seen before. He started being critical of how I looked and what I wore. He would say terrible things when we did fight that hit way below the belt. He would always apologize after, and I would forgive him, as I wanted things to work out. I also discovered, over time, a lot of hidden secrets he kept from me—big secrets, like he had claimed bankruptcy not that long before I met him, how his two sons, from his previous relationship, wanted nothing to do with him. Of course, he always had the best excuses for everything, taking no responsibility himself. He also had a younger daughter and did have a relationship with her. So, I chose to believe all the lies and excuses he told me because, once again, I wanted to be so desperately loved!

To say our relationship was turbulent would be an understatement. Greg lived with me for a year, and when things started to become abusive, I had had enough and kicked him out. But he pleaded to get back together and I wanted to believe in the "fairy-tale ending," so within months, we started dating again—this time, living apart.

You know that gut instinct we all have? Well, mine told me he was dating other women. Greg thought of himself as a real ladies' man. I never could prove it, but deep down inside I knew. This, however, did not stop me from loving him and hoping we could make a go of it. So, again, I closed my eyes and denied what I already knew. Then, unexpectedly, I became pregnant at thirty-four. I felt ready and over the moon about the news of becoming a mother. Greg was happy as well and moved back in with me to start our family.

Austin came to bless this world four weeks earlier than planned, and, boy, I couldn't have been any less prepared! I was relaxing on the couch watching one of my favourite sitcoms when I had the feeling of having to pee. Walking toward the bathroom, I felt a gush of wetness running down my legs. Damn, I've pissed myself, I thought. But in looking down at the floor, I discovered a large pool of clear fluid. Obviously, Austin was ready for his debut. This had now become full-fledged reality, and I was about to experience, physically and emotionally, the miracle of giving birth.

Greg was at work, which was forty minutes away from the hospital. So, I called on my mother-like friend, Carolyn, who wanted to be there for me and informed her that my water had broken. Suddenly, a calmness seemed to come over me that I had never experienced before.

Not knowing what was ahead of me, I slowly packed a bag and curled my hair (yeah, I know—remember, this was my first and I had no idea how soon my physical appearance would not matter in the least). Was I in for a surprise!

Once at the hospital, all were hands on deck, so to speak, and I began to feel the pain of childbirth. Greg had finally arrived at the hospital, and I had both Carolyn and Greg by my side for support. I was so grateful but scared to death!

Living in a smaller city, unfortunately, meant no decision about an epidural or not. Natural all the way, baby! I did get gas, but for all you mothers reading this, I think gas is only given to fool us into believing that it's actually going to help. After a little over eight hours, Austin made his debut. But, to be honest, by this time, you could have wrapped up a football and given it to me and I wouldn't have known the difference. After nine hours, I was exhausted.

I wish I could tell you I enjoyed the first few months of motherhood, but I didn't. From trying to heal myself after being ripped from one end to another (the doctor didn't arrive in time to do an episiotomy) and Austin constantly, inconsolably crying, I thought, What the hell have I gotten myself into?

At this time, breastfeeding was the rage and I was determined to do this for my baby. I wanted to share that blissful bonding I'd always seen on TV. No one warned me that, for us fair-haired Caucasians, this experience would be like someone giving you a jolt of shock treatment. When he latched on, I felt the twinge of pain right down to my toes! Another enjoyable moment of motherhood and I felt like a complete failure!

Finally, after two months of what seemed like never-ending torture (between lack of sleep and hearing constant crying), we discovered that Austin had colic and I, as well, wasn't producing enough milk. Once on formula, though, he was a much happier baby, and I was finally feeling myself again.

I didn't think it was possible to love another human being like this! I celebrated in awe as I watched him take his first steps and speak his first words. Feeling perhaps a little overwhelmed by this new responsibility,

I sometimes wondered while I was pregnant what happens if I don't connect with this baby. But I couldn't love him more!

In my son's first year of life, Greg and I relished all his milestones. We celebrated his first birthday by having a big party with friends and family and watched him ham it up in the spotlight. I dressed Austin like a bumble bee for his first Halloween and relished in how cute he looked. Being a mother, I finally understood why parents aren't able to show off just one picture of their precious bundle.

Unfortunately, my relationship with Greg slowly began deteriorating. I was forced to see that as much as Greg loved Austin, he was unable to commit the time needed for parenthood or our relationship. Instead, he was only focusing on being the provider and having the best lawn on the block. I could no longer turn a blind eye to his verbal insults, and we'd often yell in front of our son. I've never been the kind of girl to back down! The straw that broke the camel's back was finding out that he had strayed outside of our marriage.

The exact moment I decided to leave was when Austin, from his highchair, shouted "Stop it!" during one of our heated arguments. In that instant, I recognized the effect this unhealthy environment was having on my son. This broke my heart, and I knew what I had to do.

So, with Austin, only eighteen months old, I made one of the hardest and most terrifying decisions that I had ever made: I would leave Greg with next to no money and our future unknown.

Being a mother has taught me a valuable lesson about unconditional love and the ability to put another human being's needs before my own. I don't think I would have had the guts or courage to leave Greg without wanting more for my son, which meant leaving this toxic relationship. It was clear that if I stayed in this relationship, I would be passing the torch of dysfunction down to Austin! I wanted him to have every opportunity to become the man he was meant to be, without living in a stressful environment caused by our own unfinished business with dysfunction. Greg and I were still struggling with what had happened in our own childhood. We still hadn't dealt with our own demons before coming together as a couple. Dysfunction attracts dysfunction!

I never anticipated I would be a single mother. I already had doubts about being able to be the kind of mother to Austin that I had never had. If I was honest, had I known this was going to happen, I'm not sure that I would have chosen to become a mom and bear most of the responsibility on my own. I acquired a total new respect for women who choose to do this all on their own. I would find out just how strong my commitment was to my son. Life, at times, has a way of showing us just how strong we are capable of being.

It took me several months of feeling like someone had ripped out my heart and set it on fire before I got my act together. I once again felt abandoned and unloved; however, I was determined to give Austin a better childhood than I had—no matter what it took. It was time to break this unhealthy, unforgiving cycle, once and for all!

No one had left Greg without feeling his wrath! I will admit it didn't help that I moved out while Greg was at work, but I was scared of what he might do. In living together, I never knew what mood he was going to be in from day to day. On his good days, he was kind, but on his bad days, he was ruthless and abusive!

Before this time, my sister Gale was having difficulty with various mental illnesses. But when I had left Greg, she was on a new medication, which luckily seemed to be helping her, and she was finally feeling herself again. She lived in a two-bedroom townhouse and insisted that we stay with her until I got my feet back on the ground. Because of her generous nature, she gave up both bedrooms while she slept on a blow-up mattress downstairs in the rec room. I appreciated her support more than she'd ever know!

Within six months, we were living in our own charming, small home, which was in a family neighbourhood, close to a park. I loved this home with all its character and what it represented, as our "new beginning." I would watch Austin, now two years old, from our elevated deck, as he rode around in circles in this spacious backyard on his motorized jeep, grinning ear to ear. I felt stability now and more in control of my life than ever before.

Unfortunately for me, the more independent and stronger I grew, the more Greg became resentful of me. In his hate for me, he didn't care what consequences would follow for Austin. I would often think, why does he hate me so much? Then I came to realize later, it wasn't so much me personally but that I had the audacity to leave him. His resentment was so strong that he actually left his secure job to go live out west where his responsibility for paying child support was not enforceable because he was in a different province. Eventually Greg returned to Sarnia with back support payments now owing. Whenever Austin stayed with his dad, Greg took pleasure in putting me down, telling Austin things that weren't true. Austin returned home from these visits, upset and questioning why his father would say these things.

On one occasion, he convinced one of his girlfriends to get him a big bag of pot so he could plant it in the trunk of my car. Unbeknownst to me, he had come across one of my spare car keys after I moved out of our shared home. He knew that I went over to the States often, as I liked shopping over there, and we lived in a border city. He hoped that I would be stopped at the border and get caught with the drugs. At this time, pot was not legal, even in Canada.

When I accidentally came across the big bag of pot, I knew right away who had planted it. Now, how to prove it? It turned out that Greg's present girlfriend, who had got the pot for him, found out that he had been seeking pleasures elsewhere. As we all know, there's nothing worse than a woman scorned. So, she called me and told me what he had done. She then volunteered to go to my lawyer's office to sign an affidavit stating this, as she knew Greg was fighting for sole custody of Austin. She knew he was trying to portray me as an unfit mother. At this point, I had already spent ten thousand dollars in this fight. Knowing how damaging this information would be to his character, Greg backed off.

Never mind the terrible twos! I was proud I had sailed past this stage, but I had no clue what the next stage would bring. Now, at three years old, Austin would test my patience, endurance, and my unconditional love. I would be lying to say that dealing with this stage on my own wasn't challenging and exhausting. At times, I felt pushed to my limits, but somehow, I got through this, as most of us parents do.

Because I wanted to take advantage of Austin learning French as a second language, we moved to a new home in a district where this was offered. Austin wasn't quite four yet when I walked him into his classroom—his next milestone. Part of me felt excited about this next phase of his life and all the new discoveries that lay ahead for him. But as I left, I felt like I was leaving a part of me behind. Of course, like we all do, I drove myself nuts all day, worrying if Austin was okay. I'm surprised I didn't drive over and peek into the classroom windows. Okay, I admit, I did think about it. As all parents reading this know, this worrying about your child trumps everything and is for life—another lesson learned about parenting, which was accepted open heartedly.

I worried if Austin would be able to learn another language while still learning English, so I made sure every night at bedtime, while snuggling together, I read an English book to him—these moments became so very special to me. Having wanted to experience this myself as a child, I knew how important this time spent together would impact him and create treasured memories for his future. It was always important to me that he knew, now and forever, he was worthy of love and was so valued as a person.

For the first two years of kindergarten, Austin showed me just how quickly he could learn another language, even though we didn't speak French at home. I was so grateful to be able to give this to him.

By Grade 1, the structure of the classroom would be very different, as throw into the mix was learning every subject, all day long, in French. For all of you who have sons, I'm sure you'll agree, to get a boy at this age to sit in one spot for most of the day is expecting a lot! At the first parent–teacher meeting, I was informed by the teacher that she felt Austin needed to be tested to see if a learning disorder existed. I felt as if someone had punched me in the gut and feared what this might mean for my son now and in the future. Was somehow this my fault? After I held it together during this meeting, the tears came flooding down my face on the drive home.

At the meeting to discuss the results of the testing, Austin's teacher, principal, a woman who was head of the Learning Disabilities Association and I were all present. I was told that Austin had a "non-verbal" learning disability (NVLD) and the obstacles he would face in learning were explained. Before I spoke, the teacher recommended that he be taken out of the French immersion program, and she went on to say there had never been a child with a learning disability in this program. I don't know if it was my anger or lack of acceptance, but I wasn't prepared to take this off the table quite yet for my son. I witnessed him picking up the language, regardless of any learning issues he had. I thought, Why would I take this opportunity away from him when learning French isn't a problem? Thankfully, the woman in charge of the Learning Disabilities Association agreed with me to keep Austin in. Now, I needed to learn as much as I could about this disorder as possible. NVLD is characterised by a significant discrepancy between higher verbal skills and weaker motor, visual, spatial, and social skills. This was all overwhelming, to say the least.

Luckily for me, there was a ten-week program offered through our community that met weekly, and I jumped right in. I would now get educated about all the different types of learning disabilities. I quickly learned that there were many learning disabilities, all that came with different challenges, some so severe it was heartbreaking to hear. Some of the parents that attended these classes were exhausted, mentally and financially, due to the lack of funding for the extra care needed in the more severe cases. This gave me a reality check on how much more I could be dealing with and taught me a whole different level of compassion. So, in a nutshell, Austin needed his paperwork lessons spaced out and bigger, he needed more time for tests and would receive a laptop in Grade 5 to help him type, instead of struggling to write. I had all the confidence in the world that he would be able to deal with these obstacles and flourish in what ever areas he desired. Thankfully, I also was able to provide a tutor for him.

During these first few years of elementary school, Austin's classmates would not notice the extra help he was given, or they just didn't care. But that changed in Grade 5 when he received his laptop, which was provided by the school for children with learning disabilities. Back then, a laptop was very noticeable. As we know, children can be cruel. Some would make fun of Austin for his differences. Many times, he came home from school and I witnessed the pain on his face, though he tried his best to hide it. All I could do was stand helplessly with my arms around him, reassuring him that this would pass. At some point, there will be a time in your child's life when part of their innocence is stripped away like a dandelion on a windy day. The first time witnessing this always hurts the most, as you helplessly watch and realize you have no control to prevent this now or in the future. However, you can reinforce that they are loved and supported through whatever life brings.

On a positive note, though, Austin was picking up this second language beautifully and discovering his own strengths. He was easy going and well liked by teachers and friends. He was my reason for learning to be an advocate while I also taught him to advocate for himself. I had many talks with Austin to try and help him understand that, like him, others learned differently as well, and this would only be a detriment if he allowed it. I encouraged him to take advantage of the extra help and just do his very best. After all, that is all any of us can do!

When Austin was nine, two of us became three. I remarried and brought another person into our tightly woven twosome: Steve. Austin realized he would now have to share my attention. It took some time, but I convinced him that loving another person wouldn't diminish the love I had for him.

Over the few next years, we loved seeing Austin explore different sports and other interests. When he discovered that he excelled at football, seeing the joy and satisfaction on his face brought me such happiness. At times I felt, through Austin, I was living the childhood I once had longed for—another gift I received for being a mother.

As parents, all we can do is our best, and sometimes that means being truthful and vulnerable with our children, showing the human side that exists in us all. I understood, now, that my lack of having a stable, happy childhood helped give me the perspective and determination I needed to provide one for Austin!

Within the first year of our new family, we welcomed another—a furry four-legged friend named Coco. This adorable puppy tugged at all our heart strings, and I hoped that Austin would learn a lesson in unconditional love and the responsibility of caring and loving another living creature. Okay, I know this was wishful thinking. We all shared in loving this adorable little cutie, creating another mutual bond between us all.

Our new family unit was everything I hoped it would be—a stable and loving family environment. Unfortunately, this would be the calm before the storm!

A call came that changed our live. "I have cancer of the pancreas." It was Greg. Not that any cancer is good, but I knew the that the odds were against him. The words just came out of my mouth, "How long do you have to live?"

Greg was mortified at my lack of emotion, but unfortunately, his constant attempts to ruin and hurt me left me feeling less than sympathetic. My first thought after the shock wore off was, How the hell am I going to be able to help my son get through this very difficult time? I knew this life-changing event would impact him for the rest of his life.

They say children are resilient, and they are, but having to explain to your child that they are about to watch their dad slowly die was gut wrenching, to say the least. At such a young age, Austin was forced to deal with what would prove to be one of life's biggest challenges. For the most part, he was such a soldier through it all. I was so very moved and proud of him for being able to be there in his father's final moments of life—all at the young age of twelve. I can't imagine how difficult this would have been for him. Sometimes, life is not fair, and there's not a damn thing we can do about it!

Within a year of this news and after his father continually trying experimental treatments to stay alive longer, we got news that his aunt Gale, like a second mother, had cancer, again, for the third time. Unfortunately, like Greg's, it would be slow and painful to watch.

All I could think of was, Really, God, you're going to throw this into the mix? I was extremely close to my sister, and trying to come to terms with losing her at the same time as dealing with my son's loss proved to be overwhelming and extremely messy at times.

So, while helping my son try to navigate through losing now two of the most important people in life, I, as well, would need to find the strength to deal with losing one of the most important in mine.

Unfortunately, Austin would also have to deal with the disappointment of not being able to see his father as much as he wanted. He loved his father, flaws and all, and like most children in this situation, he wanted to spend as much time as possible with him. Greg, on the other hand, was busy with his new wife and focused on his own needs. I know Greg loved Austin as much as he possibly could, but I hated him for his selfishness. He made little effort to see him any more than usual, especially knowing he was dying. Who does this? How could he not want to spend as much time as possible with his beautiful son to create memories that would survive his passing? Greg's priority was cementing a relationship with his new wife and fulfilling his own desires. With whatever time Greg had left, he chose to take trips, including one to Disney, and never invited Austin. I just couldn't understand this, and I wasn't the only one. Sometimes, Austin would cry himself to sleep at night, not understanding why his father was making the choices he was. This was heart wrenching, and I would lay next to Austin with the only words that I could get out of my mouth without choking on them: "Your father loves you as much as he is capable." It was after saying these words that I realized how, as an adult, I was still dealing with these same issues with my own father. Sometimes, the choices we make as parents can have such devasting consequences on our children later in life.

Gale was the best aunt Austin could have ever hoped for. She had a childlike disposition and an abundance of love for Austin. They had a deep, loving bond between them. Her being a mother as well, she knew the value of spending time with a child and showing them unconditional love. Let's not forget, the never-ending ice cream—after all, she was the aunt! They always had so much fun together. In some ways, for Austin, losing Gale proved to be just as devasting as losing his father.

Two weeks before Austin's thirteenth birthday, he and I would be attending his father's funeral. While sitting through the service, my one arm around his shoulder, I waited for the breakdown, the uncontrollable tears, but none of it came. I, again, was reminded of how we all deal with grief in our own way, children included. However, I felt some concern in Austin not expressing his grief. Preparing for his father's death, Austin attended a children's program through our local hospice that offered emotional support, as well as coping skills.

Unfortunately, I felt a sense of relief knowing that, eventually, I would no longer have to deal with Greg's dysfunctional behaviour for either me or Austin. It was years after Greg's passing that I realized just how deep the wound would be from Austin losing his father. At the time, Austin had kept most of the pain inside, and I respected that he needed to deal with his loss in whatever manner he could handle, especially knowing what was coming next.

Gale was a big part of our lives and continued to be right up until her final days. She would have a sleepover weekly, and both Austin and I always looked forward to watching movies together while eating a never-ending supply of Jujubes and popcorn. I am so grateful Austin and Gale had such a special bond.

A year to the date after Austin's father's passing, we lost Gale. Gale was loved by many, and this was evident at her funeral. We, at times, would cry together, consoling one another. I reminded Austin of how lucky we were to have had her in our lives. Nothing could ever replace that hole we both felt in our hearts.

In Grade 9 ,Austin was entering into yet another, a new phase of his life. Unfortunately, due to all the losses he had suffered in such a short amount of time, he slowly withdrew from most of his friends, as well as from me. The next thing I knew, he and I would be doing a not-so-graceful dance with a demon called Eating Disorder.

Looking back, the signs were there well before it became a crisis, as when I'd clean the Austin's bathroom, I would see traces left of dry vomit under the toilet seat. When questioned, he would simply say he had an upset stomach. I bought into his explanation, realizing he had dealt with so much loss over the past year.

Austin now refused to eat meals with us. His clothes that once fit snugly now hung off his body. I felt helpless not knowing how to deal with this, and unfortunately, I found there was little support available besides a biweekly meeting with a counsellor. I guess this would be better than nothing. I witnessed my son, who once would have been considered overweight at 220 pounds, drop down to 138 pounds at a height of six foot two. I was mortified that I could see Austin's spine.

I screamed, I cried, and I begged him to start eating. I even threatened to take away his Xbox, hoping it would be an easy to fix. As I learned over the year, this disorder was more about having control over something than it was about eating. We learned a lot on this journey together and, at times, had to step back from one another. I prayed and hoped that he would find his way back. Thank God, eventually, Austin was able to find the strength and courage to move past this terrible disease. Through my journey with him, I learned of the excruciating pain felt by parents who witness their child doing harm to themselves, in whatever manner this might be. I can now relate to the conversations we have with ourselves, asking what we did or didn't do that could have prevented this. It was a reminder of just how fragile life can be.

In Grade 12, Austin had a few girlfriends and eventually became involved in a more serious relationship. I, however, shifted from being the number one woman in his life to second place. I'll be honest and say, like most mothers of sons, this was a difficult adjustment. After all, I had been his everything for years. However, I recognized a long time ago, that our relationship would always be evolving, and so I decided that before he graduated high school, over spring break, we would share the trip of a lifetime together. We hadn't travelled since Austin was five, when we went to Disney World. Even though I didn't have the money, I justified that it was probably the last opportunity to travel together, just the two of us, before he was out on his own. Luckily, my supportive husband, Steve, understood my reasoning for wanting to do this and wished us happy travels—another reason why I love this man, as he continually shows me how supportive he is.

Between us, we chose to visit England, Scotland, and, lastly, Iceland. I was so excited, and even though I knew Austin didn't recognize what a trip of a lifetime this was, I knew how valuable these memories would be to him later on in his life.

So off we went, discovering different countries together and all that they offered. In England, at age seventeen, Austin was of legal drinking age, so we would dine together in the pubs, eating local dishes while he enjoyed a pint. I am so glad I was able to share this first with him.

We visited Buckingham Palace and watched the changing of the guards, took a cruise down the River Thames, and bought souvenirs to remind us of this country and all its beautiful landmarks. Next, we enjoyed the four-hour train ride from London to Edinburgh, Scotland.

We were both in awe of the beauty of the landscape while making this journey. Edinburgh had a feel of its own, offering a mysterious castle, museums, and quaint local shops to visit. We both loved the feel of this much smaller place than London, England. From our hotel window, we could see in the distance, the big mysterious castle, waiting to be explored. When it was time to leave, we were both sad that we didn't have more time to explore.

Last, but not least, we flew into Iceland, excited about our next adventure. We instantly sensed a totally different vibe there. The homes were scattered on beautiful, spacious lots, where neighbours were seen at a distance. Many natural hot springs and hard black lava appeared throughout much of area. The Blue Lagoon, the most famous hot spring in the world, was an experience like no other. I had to book this day-excursion well in advance, as through our research, we knew it would be a once-in-a-lifetime experience. The dining room, which was built with huge, tall glass walls, enabled guests to see this steamy wonder while enjoying succulent food in a fluffy bathrobe. I had never experienced anything in my previous travels like this—and it was magical.

Upon returning to Canada, I was exhausted. Three countries in ten days took a toll on my body, but I was glad to be home. I found it strange that Austin's girlfriend was waiting in the driveway, but I recognized and remembered the intensity of my "first love." However, within three days of our returning home, without warning, Austin packed his things in a big garbage bag and said that he was leaving to go live with her and her family. I was blindsided. Austin's reasoning for this was he wasn't happy living with us anymore.

I felt as though someone had ripped my heart out, as well as thinking, You ungrateful . . . Well, you get the picture.

For six weeks, Austin refused to return my calls or text messages, making this even more unbearable. I knew that this stage in adolescence could and would be challenging, but I wasn't prepared for this. I sank into a depression, which brought me to my knees. How could my only child do this to me? I had invested so much time and love in our relationship—where did I go wrong? My husband, along with close friends, assured me I was a great mom, but these words did little to console me. I felt completely crushed.

Austin's graduation ceremony arrived, and I wasn't going to let his actions prevent me from seeing this milestone event. Steve and I sat high in the bleachers where I could barely see him, but I was glad I was there. I texted him and let him know we had come and asked if we could meet up with him after the ceremony. We searched, and Austin was no where to be found. I cried all the way home, thinking how and why he would treat me this way.

So, with no other choice, I waited patiently for him to go through, figure out, and deal with whatever it was he needed to do. After all, what was I going to do? Go over there and physically force him to come home? I felt the need to write Austin a letter, letting him know that although I didn't understand what he was going through, I loved him and would always be here for him.

Finally, after three months and what seemed like an eternity, Austin came home. With time, realization can occur. The novelty of being independent, away from us, while with another family, eventually showed Austin that home wasn't so bad after all. Although I forgave him, I made it clear that it would take a long time for me to rebuild the trust I once had. Another lesson he needed to learn: actions have consequences.

Through our many conversations, I would come to realize that Austin was still dealing with all his losses; he was still angry at life's unfairness. He was coming to terms with just how much his actions had hurt me and deeply apologized. You know the saying, "You always hurt the ones you love." Our relationship, yet again, was evolving to a different place that was unfamiliar to the both of us.

I reflected on what I had learned from this event and came to recognize that, for whatever reason, Austin was unable to sort his stuff out while at home. He had an opportunity to leave, and he did. As much as this hurt me, I came to recognize it wasn't about me. That sometimes, in people's lives, space is required to do their own healing. This can mean temporarily walking away. Now, don't get me wrong, in this case, I did not feel this was an acceptable way for him to handle this, but still, it happened. Now dealing with our emotions, it was time for healing and rebuilding our relationship.

As you know, no one can hurt you like your child. I've asked myself on many occasions, why is this? My own conclusion is that it's because of the overwhelming, unconditional love we have for this human that we brought into this world.

In the following few years, Austin completed a two-year program at our local college in Police Foundation. I was so proud of him, making this commitment and finishing. Unfortunately for me, as fate would have it, I yet again would not be getting any graduation pictures, as he chose not to attend the ceremony. I didn't like his decision but respected it. I realized this was not about what I wanted.

While attending college, Austin was hired on at Wow, selling cell phones and plans. Once finished school, he was given a full-time position, as they quickly learned that he was a natural at customer service. It's such a fulfilling experience to watch your child become an adult as they discover the gifts they posses.

I've learned through being a parent and observing others that regardless of how much time or love you put into parenting, there is no guarantee on the outcome. We do the best we can and hope that our children find their own true path, making the world a better place in their own unique way. We come to recognize how important those mistakes our children make are and necessary to help them learn and grow. Perhaps the biggest lesson we learn is what a gift unconditional love can be—that from it, we can learn so much about ourselves.

You, Austin, now and forever, will always be my greatest gift received.

CHAPTER 7

Little Did I Know

I had no idea in meeting my husband, Steve, all those years ago, how much I would come to need his support and unconditional love in the years to come.

After being a single mom for seven years, I finally met a man with a sense of humour and, most importantly, who knew how to treat a woman with respect and sensitivity. How I met him was not how I would have ever imagined. Through a colleague at my RE/MAX I was convinced to meet this "great guy." How many times have we women heard this before? I replied, "If he's so great, then why is he still single?"

I agreed to meet him for a coffee at Tim Horton's and had a backup plan in place in case things went south. Being in real estate gave me an easy out. I could simply say I had an appointment if I felt I needed to escape. With a coffee in hand at a table for four, I waited for my friend, Patti, to arrive with Steve. Little did I know Steve was already here, waiting at another table. We had no idea what each other looked like, although I had a hard time believing that. My face had been advertised throughout our local city papers. I saw Patti enter through the doors and watched as she walked over to where Steve was sitting. As they both made their way over to my table, I gave Steve a quick once over. He was medium built and was much taller than me and had a boyish look about him. I knew he was in his late forties and worked for Canadian National Railway. Him having a decent job was a prerequisite for me.

At this stage of my life, I was not interested in supporting anyone else, thank you.

Once the introductions were done, Patti left us on our own. It was quite obvious he was losing his hair on the top of his head and had the "swoop" thing going on. I thought, Man, just shave it all off. Within a month of dating, I suggest he just part with it all, finding out later in our relationship that his hairdresser had wanted to do this for years.

To my surprise, talking came easily, and we enjoyed each other's company. When I really had to go, Steve walked me to my car, and after I unlocked it, he opened the door for me. Okay, now I was impressed, as manners are important to me. He now had my attention, and I agreed to give him my number.

Our first date, however, almost never happened. At the last minute, I had to cancel because my son, Austin, was sick. Much later in our relationship, I discovered Steve almost decided not to make that second call, thinking he was being blown off. Luckily for us, he made that call. I guess it was our destiny to meet at this stage of life. I know, in my earlier years, I wouldn't have given Steve a second look because I was nowhere ready to appreciate all that he had to offer. I was still working out my own stuff. I was much more superficial in my younger years and would not have even considered dating a man going bald. I learned he had been on his own for eighteen years and wondered why. Does he have hidden issues? I questioned, still not trusting that this man might be the real deal. I learned he was not prepared to just settle for the sake of companionship. I respected him for this. For me, enough years had passed, and I felt ready now to take that plunge back into the pool of love.

Steve quickly realized that having a relationship with me meant he was also taking on a relationship with my son, Austin. He needed to fit into our lives, so to speak. I made it quite clear, that my first priority was Austin. Without hesitation, he told me he understood and respected me for this. I found this heartwarming, especially as Steve was not a parent himself but could understand my priorities. The more time we spent together, the closer we became. Austin liked him, and I welcomed the bond they were creating. We thoroughly enjoyed acting like teenagers again, having sex whenever and wherever we could. He not only knew how to treat a woman but also knew how to please a woman. We fell in love.

Within a year, we were married and had our new family. Our first year was filled with adjustments and expectations, but lots of love. I often wondered, if he knew what was around the corner, would he have still married me?

I no longer felt threatened by Austin's father, as I now had Steve by my side when dealing with Greg's drama and personal attacks. I felt my life was finally calm and grounded, having no idea what was yet to come.

When the unexpected call came of Greg telling us he had pancreas cancer, Steve was there for us. But then while helping Austin deal with watching his father slowly die, I would get the news that my sister Gale was having to fight, yet, another battle with cancer. She was my best friend, my biggest cheerleader, and the closest relationship I had to a mother—how the hell was I going to deal with all of this? I instinctively went into my survival mode.

Over the next two years, before the passing of Greg and Gale, Steve watched helplessly as I spiralled out of control. Our relationship, for me, now moved down the "totem pole," so to speak. I continued to act like a single warrior, as this was all I knew. I hadn't yet experienced a committed, loving relationship with a man who was willing to stay through some of my darkest days.

My reckless behaviour included sometimes staying out all night drinking and getting high with a male friend I had known since childhood. Even though Steve knew he was only a friend, this cut him to the core, as he realized I was emotionally leaning on someone other than him.

One night, I said to Steve, "Look, if you can't deal with all of this, I understand. You can leave."

I think subconsciously I was sabotaging our relationship, as I believed his leaving would happen eventually anyway. With a horrified look on his face, Steve calmly replied, "I love you and I'm not going anywhere."

Talk about unconditional love! I know if he was handling his own crisis in this manner, I think I would have thrown his sorry ass to the curb.

This, my friend, is what is called unconditional love. Steve had no judgement or resentment toward me while I was in this fragile state. He sat quietly in the background and offered strength and tenderness when I reached out. He chose to stay while I was in my "hot mess," rooting for the real me to survive it all.

I am so grateful that we survived this. Steve loved me enough and chose to accept my "checking out," hoping, one day, the woman he fell in love with would resurface. Looking back, I now realize how much I needed professional help. I was still living with my own life's wounds that continued oozing out. Up until now, all I knew was to sink or swim on my own.

Marriage is like a rollercoaster. At times, it is so intoxicating, as we move and grow together. At other times, when facing life's obstacles, we may feel the need to "dine and dash"!

I am so grateful that finally in my life, I have danced with most of my demons and have now created my own new "dance card." Every now and then, they try to resurface, but I remind them this dance has already been taken!

CHAPTER 8

A Letter to Coco

Dear Coco,

As I lay beside you, stroking your head and back while you are basking in the sun streaming in from the window, I wonder how many more of these moments will we have.

You became part of our family at seven weeks old, and weighing only three and a half pounds, you looked like a miniature Ewok. I immediately saw your feistiness and need for control, as you would constantly push your brothers and sisters of your way. Your colouring stood out, as your siblings were blends of black and white, but you, on the other hand, were a beautiful colour of a sandy beach mixed with cocoa. As I stood above the dog pen, where room to run was scarce, I was drawn to pick you up. As I held you in the palm of my hand and looked into your deep brown eyes, I instantly fell in love.

My son, Austin, and I had been looking at puppies on and off for months. Let's face it, all puppies are cute. Observing me, the lady working in the pet store came over to the clinch the sale, so to speak. She said you were a Lhasa Apso and came with a heavy price tag of $650. In 2006, that was a hefty price. She wanted me to make the decision there and then, reminding me that you may not be here the following morning. I explained to her I planned to return with Austin, as I wanted him to be involved in this decision of picking our newest family member.

We already had an eleven-year-old cat named Rex, who was dearly loved and had been part of Austin's life since he was a baby. But it was time for another life-changing connection, one with a new puppy. Little did I know the commitment involved or what I was exactly getting into.

My husband and I had discussed that if we were going to make this commitment, we would do it while Austin was young, as we planned to have him involved with the responsibilities that go along with having a dog—okay, at least this was the plan. So, I made the decision that if you were indeed the one, you would still be there when I returned with Austin in the morning.

Austin couldn't wait to meet you. As soon as he held you, he instantly fell in love and our decision was made. Never buying a puppy before, I quickly discovered all the "must haves" that go along with this decision, and total investment was $980. Yikes!

Steve had known we had been looking on an off for a puppy for a while now and had hoped that our decision would not be made until the warmer weather, obviously for potty training reasons. However, it was only the end of January and very cold, with a lot of snow. As Steve walked through the front door that evening after finishing his afternoon shift, I am sure you were the last thing he expected to see.

We lived in an open-concept, one-floor home, and as soon as Steve entered, you were in full view. I was sitting on our sectional couch with a look that would be a dead give away in a poker game. I was a little nervous, due to not preparing Steve for your arrival, but as I predicted, he, as well, fell instantly in love with you, especially your cute underbite.

I had never trained a puppy before, and you tested my patience, understanding, and forgiveness. Being a mother definitely was helpful, especially for those times when I was on the phone and saw you peeing on the floor while looking at me, not understanding what the cute bells hanging off the door were for. In your first year, you seemed hellbent on digging at night, especially in my favourite chair. This would test, even more, my ability to forgive. There were times I definitely thought, What the hell did I get myself into?

During the daytime, you felt the need to eat anything you could find and then regurgitate it all over the carpet, the floor being too easy to clean up. During these beginning stages of your life, we still had no idea how strong the shared bond of unconditional love would be with you.

I came to learn that dogs are creatures of habit, somewhat like a child. They like routine—and especially to be fed on time! If your schedule wasn't kept, you would let me know by your pacing in and out of the kitchen. I loved taking walks with you and seeing how happy this made you. At times, it appeared you were smiling! For many years, when nighttime fell, our own special routine would be you jumping up next to me on the couch. You waited patiently for my tender strokes, responding with kisses, creating an even deeper bond between us. Our time together—me unwinding from the day and you with a full belly of dinner and treats—made me feel grateful for this special bond we share.

Through one of your routine vet visits, we received devastating news: tumours were growing in your lung. The veterinarian showed us the X-ray and the three little dot-like images. She explained there was no way to tell how quickly or slowly these tumours would grow. I cried all the way home, already starting the grieving of what was to come. Our time left for Coco was unknown.

I could see now through the shortening of our walks together that your little body was showing me just how far you could go. Our once fast-paced twenty-minute stride was now a ten-minute leisurely stroll. When I was at home, your need to be near me became more of a necessity for you, following me from room to room. At night, when you were fast asleep, I heard more wheezing in your breathing. As sad as it was to accept the inevitable, I was grateful, due to a lull in my business, I had been able to spend more time with you at home.

Months after your diagnosis, we learned that the veterinarian, who had been involved with your care for the past few years, had relocated. We needed to look for a new vet. It was not the best time in your life to switch vets, but we chose one that was highly recommended. Steve and I were both present at your first checkup. Your records were transferred to the new office, and we discussed with the new vet what options were available regarding your tumours. After his examination of your X-ray, the new vet thought it was best to have it read by a radiologist in order to confirm the previous diagnosis.

Now having a window of hope, we waited restlessly until results were in. Steve and I were present with you at the vet's office, hoping to hear good news. To our surprise, we were told you, in fact, did not have tumours growing in your lungs after all. Thankfully, you were not leaving us any time soon. We cried tears of relief but were also upset that we had been told differently, as for months now we had all been trying to come to terms with the loss we were about to experience.

I guess, at the end of the day, this was a reminder that medicine is not an exact science, and sometimes mistakes are made. I couldn't wait to tell Austin the great news. Luckily, we are still enjoying more time with you.

I now realize why I believed you were dying earlier, not just because we were told but indeed old age was taking its toll. You had gone through several surgeries and numerous ongoing ear and skin infections. Years of taking medicine to treat the infections was harming your now frail body. We noticed you were sleeping more and more and wanted walks less. We couldn't love you more, but financially, it was taking a toll. When you were thirteen, going on fourteen, we made a decision for your remaining days. No more surgeries or drugs, other than those to keep you comfortable. For all you dog owners, you know that nobody knows your dog like you do. We all know when our four-legged friends need this help. We left it in God's hands.

I'm so glad you came into our lives all those years ago, not just to love and entertain us, but to teach us just how meaningful our connection to dogs can be, to remind us to slow down and take in those moments that pass so quickly but mean so much. Above all, you gave your unconditional love to us, without any judgement or agenda . . . okay maybe for a treat or two.

My dear friend, companion and confidant, I would not have missed our relationship for anything. Although the cost of loving you will leave a hole in my heart forever, I know one day I will see you again. I will forever cherish all the unconditional love that you gave us in your own special way!

CHAPTER 9

Gale and Butterflies

As I hurriedly drive to the hospice to pick up my sister Gale, for dinner and a visit, I recognized that any day could be her last. She had been there for two weeks, and because of her remarkable sunny disposition, I think the staff as well as volunteers found it hard to believe that she was close to dying. At times, hell, I even fooled myself into believing different.

As I walked down the hallway toward her room, I could hear faint sounds of sobbing. As I entered her room, there Gale was, sitting on the edge of her bed. When I asked her what was wrong, she said, "I don't know if you know how much you mean to me." I replied, tears now streaming down my face, "Yes, I do because I feel the exact same way about you." Little did I know, these words would be one of my last memories before she slipped into a peaceful coma that evening and passed on thirty-six hours later. I am so grateful, now, that we were able to share this moment without even realizing just how close her departure would be.

Unfortunately for Gale, right from the beginning, my mother lacked any maternal or loving feelings for her. I remember as a child wondering why our mother seemed to have so much anger toward Gale. She was the oldest of four, seven years older than me, and she was expected to step up and take care of us when my mother wasn't able to, which unfortunately was most of the time, due to her severe depression.

I can only imagine how overwhelming this was for a teenager. She did it lovingly as, even then, her nature was to love and nurture.

From my earliest memories, Gale was kind, non-judgemental, and there for me while we were living together in our dysfunctional family home. One memory that comes to mind was lying together on a blanket in our backyard, sunbathing and singing along to music from her small AM/FM radio. With our mother actually out of the house, Gale took advantage of this and used her bottle of "Sun In," a product that back then was a popular, affordable highlighter for your hair. Even though I had white-blonde hair, Gale still included me, spraying it in both our hair. As a child I knew, if my mother ever found out about this, Gale would have faced terrible consequences. She always made a point of letting me know that I mattered and that she cared. Our special bond would be something like no other and continued to deepen over the years.

Luckily for Gale, in high school, she was well liked, due to her outgoing personality, and quickly made friends. She met three sisters who also attended there. Unfortunately, they had lost their mother at a young age, but thankfully, they had a rock-solid, loving father. Once he was aware of Gale's situation at home, he welcomed her to come live with them. At the age of sixteen, Gale moved into their home when my mother left my father and moved away, taking the three of us along with her to another city. I'm sure Gale was sad to watch her sisters and brother leave but was thankful she was going to live in a more supportive, loving environment.

While in high school, Gale was able to enjoy many activities and was also able to date, which was previously not allowed by my mother. My pretty blonde-haired, green-eyed sister was finally getting some happiness. She eventually attracted the attention of a young man named Mark. They quickly fell in love and were married within a year.

Mark was an ambitious young man and started a refrigeration and cooling business, something he was familiar with, as his father was also in the business. This proved to offer some financial stability for them. Gale was also working full time as a secretary, and within a few years, they bought their first home. They purchased a duplex and made their living quarters in the top unit while renting out the bottom; they were both excited about their first financial investment.

At that time, four years had passed since I had the opportunity to see my older sister. Finally, at twelve, living with my father and stepmother, I could visit her, travelling by train. I was living in Hamilton, three hours away from Gale in Sarnia. Saving up my babysitting money, I used it to travel to Sarnia as often as I could. I always looked forward to the fun we shared together, as well as her supportive, loving nature. I was entering into womanhood and, without a mother, needed this more than ever.

At age fifteen, I looked older than I was being well endowed and wearing makeup. On one visit, Gale included me with her friends to go to a local bar, where I tried my first Brown Cow—so yummy. I felt included in her tight-knit group of friends. Back then, you weren't asked for ID, especially if you were with one of "the regulars."

It seemed Gale was always looking for a new challenge, and with her love of people, she started selling Mary Kay part time—and she blossomed. Her ability to connect enthusiastically with women, introducing them to skincare and makeup, was contagious. She loved helping women feel beautiful. She introduced Mary Kay to me, as well, and taught me, at a young age, the importance of taking care of my skin. Now that I am getting older, I appreciate her guidance even more.

The summer I was nineteen, I experienced another one of life's bumps in the road. I had been fired from a retail job and was devastated, as I had never been fired before. Gale generously offered to let me stay all summer with her and her husband at their home in Sarnia. As Mark had his own business, he hired me on to be a receptionist—let's not forget the money I so desperately needed.

During my stay, Gale insisted on taking me to a Mary Kay Seminar, which was basically a weekend gala in Toronto. I was in awe of all the glamour and excitement. I had never experienced anything like that before and soaked up all of the positive energy from what seemed like thousands of Mary Kay reps wearing pink, including the lady herself. It turned out to be a weekend for the books for sure.

Before returning home after this fun-filled summer, Gale shared with me that she was pregnant. I congratulated her with mixed emotions. I was happy for her but knew this precious little human would take up more of her time and be more of a priority than me. Well, at least that's what I thought.

The arrival of her daughter, Michelle, on July 12, 1979, was much anticipated by all. As soon as I held her in my arms, I instantly fell in love. I had never been around many babies up until now and really didn't know what to expect. But the love I shared for my sister was now even more special thanks to this bundle of joy. Gale, now a new mother, taught me a valuable life lesson: there are many different faces of unconditional love, and just because a new one enters, does not make any others less valuable or treasured. For me, this little blonde, blue-eyed girl would now take a place in my heart forever. Unfortunately, in the not-too-distant future, Gale's blissful happiness was about to come to a screeching halt.

One day, as the tunes played loudly in my car, I eased into the two-hour drive to Sarnia. I couldn't wait to see my sister. For whatever reason, I had this uncomfortable feeling in the pit of my stomach. Not understanding why, I chose simply to ignore it. After all, what could possibly be wrong? I was on my way to one of my favourite places on earth.

As I pulled into the driveway and noticed shattered glass scattered all over the ground outside of the side entrance, that gnawing feeling resurfaced in full force. My heart pounded rapidly as I reached to pull the shattered screen door open and more glass fell out. I entered cautiously and yelled out my sister's name. I heard nothing back. With all the curtains drawn and the house in an unsettling dark disarray, I just knew something was very wrong. As I looked around, it eerily felt like time had somehow stood still in this space. Where were Gale and the baby? She knew I was coming. Had someone broken in? I slowly walked down the hallway that led to the bedrooms, coming to Michelle's room first. As I looked in, there Michelle lay, sound asleep, in her crib. Thank God! Now where was Gale? As I approached the entrance to her bedroom, in full view, there she was, sitting on the edge of her bed, just staring blankly out the open window.

"Hi," I said. "Are you okay?" She got up and hugged me, long and hard. I could sense her overwhelming sadness. "What happened to the side door?" I asked. Gale's nature was one of hiding away all the dirty little details of what was going wrong with her life. She was human after all, but this time, she would need to share.

Her marriage was falling apart. Like the broken pieces of glass that lay outside the home, some things just can't be put back together again. Mark and Gale tried, but too much damage had happened already.

One thing Gale and Mark had in common was they both liked to drink. Not surprisingly, at this time, Gale came to lean on this crutch even more. On one occasion, Gale experienced a blackout while two-year-old Michelle was in her care. This jolted Gale into a realization: it was time to put her daughter's welfare first and quit drinking. Clarity followed, as Gale came to terms that she and Mark no longer had drinking as a common bond. Within months of giving up alcohol, the marriage ended.

Since Mark was the main "bread earner," Gale's lifestyle dramatically changed. No longer living in her once beloved, cozy bungalow near a park and steps away from a beautiful, sandy beach, she moved to the upper unit of their duplex, which had become a rental property. Gale had Michelle living with her while she and Mark tried to agree on terms of their separation.

Unfortunately, coping with the care of Michelle would prove to be challenging, due to Gale's discovery of her mental illness. She wasn't sure if this was inherited from our mother or was developed due to all the stresses in life she had already dealt with.

It was just a matter of time before Mark discovered Gale's declining mental state and sought and obtained full custody of their daughter Michelle, now three. Unfortunately, forty years ago, there was still little understanding of all the different types of mental illnesses, never mind the huge stigma attached. At that time, some treatments were still experimental. The cards were stacked against Gale, so to speak. The consequences of losing custody of her daughter were devastating and escalated her mental illness to new heights.

One day, Gale walked into her favourite coffee shop and ordered her usual. She sat down for a few minutes and, out of no where it seemed, stood up and started screaming. With little understanding or compassion, a customer immediately called the police. Fear is such a powerful emotion and can cause us to react without proper assessment of some situations. While people waited for the police to come, most stayed to see the show play out.

Gale then walked outside the establishment and started doing cartwheels in the middle of the road. When the police arrived, they, too, had little knowledge or training on how to deal with mental illness, so into the back of the cruiser, handcuffed, she went. Destination? The "Mental Ward" at our local hospital.

I had never been in this ward before, and when I visited her, I was mortified. For the first twenty-four hours, she was put in a straight jacket and locked up in a small cement room, with only a mattress on the floor and no visitors allowed. I am not sure about you, but I found this extreme and cruel. Was this how our medical system helped the weakest and most vulnerable in our society? My heart felt heavy with pain and sadness. I so desperately wanted to take Gale, whom I loved so much, out of here.

I later discovered that she had stopped taking the medication she had been prescribed, as Gale found it to be of no help. I learned, unfortunately, people go through many trials of different medications before, hopefully, finding one that helps. Statistics show that as much as thirty percent of people with mental illness have no response at all to any medication. This shocked me. It would take Gale almost twenty-five years before finally finding medication that helped her.

Over her years of battling mental illnesses, schizophrenia, and depression, Gale had some pockets of time where she was able to function. She did not waste these precious moments. Gale went to college to learn about computers and, two years later, graduated. I attended her graduation and couldn't have been prouder and happier for her. Unfortunately, shortly after accomplishing this, she endured another breakdown. Usually, at these times, she would isolate herself, sometimes for months. Living in Sarnia now, I wanted to help but found it was impossible. Each time she went through an episode, I felt the loss of our relationship and never felt so helpless in my life.

At this time, my father was running his own real estate company and I worked for him. When Gale was well enough, she wanted to join in on the passion both myself and our father had for real estate. So once again, she took the bull by the horns and got her real estate licence. She was a natural. People were drawn to her sunny disposition, and it was evident how much she loved it. Unfortunately, she only got to enjoy her new profession for six months before yet another breakdown!

I was so in awe of her resilience and determination time and time again. She continually showed me just how strong she was, despite the ongoing episodes of her mental illness.

Gale first received news she had breast cancer at the young age of thirty-four, and back in the early nineties, that was unheard of. At this time, Gale was living in Toronto, trying so desperately to live independently and build a life of her own. With her diagnosis, Gale, unfortunately, came to discover she had to have a mastectomy. Since she had little money and no car, she had no choice but to return to Sarnia after her surgery. Being back in Sarnia made her life a lot less stressful, as she had the support of family and friends while she recuperated. Some of her friends brought her meals and gave her much needed company while my father gave her financial support.

Gale remained cancer free for ten years, until it reared its ugly head again at age forty-three. She knew too well what lay ahead of her as she received the news. Her other breast would now have to be removed. Since I was close, I was able to help her and would assist her to the necessary doctor's appointments. I made sure she knew I had her back.

On one occasion, while helping her get undressed, I was horrified to see the scars left behind, which were a constant reminder of all her battles with cancer. I, myself, wondered if the loss of both of her breasts made her feel any less of a woman. Personally, I think I would have been angry and wallowed in my own self-pity, wondering, why me? However,

Gale never showed any of these emotions to me and seemed to just keep going, so grateful to still be alive.

My sister was the fun aunt for all her nieces and nephews. In some ways, she was a big kid herself. She loved candy and ice cream and had no fear of being silly and totally herself. My son, Austin, and Gale shared such a special bond. She always made the effort to spend quality time with him when well enough. She was like a second mother; I knew there wasn't anything she wouldn't do for him. I was so grateful they shared this close relationship.

Over the next thirteen years of being cancer free, Gale accepted she could no longer hold a job, due to never knowing when her mental illness would kick in. However, she volunteered when able and was especially committed to the Organization for Literacy in Lambton. Helping others regardless of her own circumstances was just in her DNA.

Six months before her passing, Gale was recognized by this literacy organization, receiving a beautiful, local hand-painted painting in recognition of her years of contribution. I, again, was in awe of her ability to help others, regardless of what she was facing herself, always grateful for the times when she could function and contribute to others.

Gale's daughter, Michelle, was living in San Francisco. As she became older, Michelle was able to let go of the resentment she felt in her teens toward her mother's illness. Now a nurse, she was able to understand that mental illness is disease; from this, she began the healing process and forgive her mother's past behaviours. She and Gale, sadly, only were able to enjoy this new relationship over the span of a few years.

As fate would have it, just months before Gale's next cancer diagnosis, she and I flew out to San Francisco for a visit with Michelle. I stayed a week and Gale for two. Little did Michelle and I know how much these memories shared would come to mean. Michelle was the perfect hostess, taking us to some of San Francisco's well-known sites and out for amazing food. Upon arriving home, Michelle surprised both Gale and I with a photo album, filled with pictures we had taken while sharing these special moments.

The third time, in this case, was not a charm. Cancer had returned, yet again, this time in her lymph nodes and in her liver. We knew, this time, she could not defeat this relentless disease.

Gale was now living in hospice, and so I was grateful that she was in such a beautiful, supportive environment. At the same time, I felt overwhelmed with the sense of loss yet to come. Seeing Gale's strength and positive outlook, I just never dreamed that this disease would actually take her. This time, the cancer was in her lymph nodes and would eventually take over her body. There was no more that could be done.

At two a.m., I received a call letting me know that Gale's time was close. My husband, Steve, drove me to be with her to spend these final moments by her side. She was now unconscious, but I stayed, lying in a cot beside her bed, holding her hand through the night. I talked to her, hoping she could hear me, letting her know I was there. When morning arrived, I called Michelle to give her the sad news. She booked the soonest available flight, but unfortunately arrived two hours too late. I had hoped that Michelle would have this time to say goodbye before her mother's passing. But it was not to be.

Once again, a reminder to me that we just never know when the last time with our loved one will be. Thankfully, Michelle, just four weeks prior, had flown to Sarnia to help and be with her mother. Gale and Michelle were aware, because of the distance between them, that this very well could be their last time together.

I had never witnessed anyone die before, especially someone that I loved so much. I am now so grateful that I was able to be there, stroking her hair, tears streaming uncontrollably down my face, while saying goodbye. Before her final breaths, I instinctively told her it was okay to go and I would see her soon. I lost a little piece of my heart that day.

My sister was my hero. Her constant resilience in life was to be admired. Gale was the first to teach me the true meaning of unconditional love: not to judge anyone for their actions but, rather, try to understand their circumstances. Her soul was kind and loving, with a childlike quality. Above all else, Gale taught me, and all who knew her, what a gift life was and to always dance like no one was watching!

Till we meet again, my sister, and continue our dance, I hope you know how much I love you and miss you every day.

CHAPTER 10

Finding the Silver Lining

The August long weekend of 2013 will be a memory etched in my mind forever. In the summer months, my husband, Steve, and I like to go to the horse races. We both love horses and are in awe of these beautiful animals as we watch them race to win. Neither one of us would have "bet" on what was to happen next.

My cell phone rang, and the words that I heard from my son's lips instantly sent wave of panic through every fiber of my being.

"Mom, the house is on fire!"

I thought I misheard. As he repeated himself, I could hear firetrucks in the background. I felt like I was in an episode of The Twilight Zone. Could this really be happening?

"Are you okay? Did you get Coco out?" I could hear the fear and state of shock he was in and said, "Just hang in there, buddy. We're on our way!"

While I was talking to Austin, Steve heard the words "house on fire" and immediately jumped into action. He raced to get to his truck. Now off the phone, I ran up what seemed to be endless stairs and pushed open the doors to the bright outside. The entrance was up high, overlooking the parking lot, and I saw Steve's green truck moving. I couldn't believe my eyes. Did he really just leave without me?

Now in a state of shock and panic, I thought, How am I going to get home? There sat an older woman on a nearby bench, smoking. I am sure she saw the look of horror on my face, and I quickly told her my dilemma. Realizing time was of the essence, she offered to help, as her car was there. It seemed like an eternity before I could finally hear clunking sounds slowly approaching the top of the hill where I stood. Her car looked like a woman's version of Uncle Buck's car, right out of the movie. I was thankful, though, and didn't care what she was driving. I went to jump in, and to my surprise, she stepped out of the driver's seat and handed me the keys.

"I'm not from around here, so you can drive." There was a split second where I thought, Should I really be driving in my panicked state? But, without a doubt, I would have walked on glass to get home.

While I was driving and giving her directions on how to get back to the horse track, she said, "Did you know the ATM machine isn't working at the track and I only brought forty dollars?"

I didn't clue in at first, but then realized she was hitting me up for money. In total disbelief, I asked myself, How could this woman really be asking me for money in my current state? At this point, I couldn't wait to get out of this car!

As we approached my street, it was blocked off by several fire trucks. Pulling off to the side of the road, I quickly got out and thanked her, nevertheless. Now, running toward my home, through the crowd of onlookers, I searched frantically for Austin. I've never hugged him so tightly or for so long. Now that I knew he was safe, my eyes locked on where Steve was standing.

"What the fuck were you thinking?" I wanted to shout, but at that moment, I realized he wasn't. He was in shock as well and had acted on impulse and adrenaline.

By the time I saw my home, the garage door had been removed and the opening had been boarded up like a bandage on a wound. Nighttime was approaching, and for obvious reasons, the hydro had been turned off in the home.

The neighbours were now heading back to their homes. The show was over. It looked to me like most of the damage occurred in the garage. Little did I know just how much smoke can destroy the interior and contents of your home.

The firemen didn't want anyone to enter our home because of the toxic fumes; however, I pleaded my way back in, just for a few minutes, to gather some clothes and necessities. It was so dark inside, and I had to use a flashlight to help find things. The feeling of eeriness was unsettling. As I shone my light on different surfaces to gather clothes and essentials, I couldn't help but notice an invasion of thick black soot, which seemed to be everywhere.

We were left to find a hotel that would accommodate the three of us and our dog, Coco. Finally, after several rejections because of having a dog, the receptionist at the Holiday Inn sympathized with our situation and made an exception, but only for one night.

Once in our room, we all collapsed in the closest seat and sat in silence, feeling a sense of numbness. None of us realized the emotional roller coaster ride that would follow.

The guys had only the clothes on their backs, and as I began to unpack, I realized so did I. The clothes that I had pulled from my dresser were covered in black soot and stunk, along with everything else I had brought.

Morning came, and we all awoke hoping that this had just been a bad dream. Our first step was to meet the insurance adjustor at our home. As I approached the house, it looked so broken, like it had been in a fight and lost. My car, which had been in the garage, was now parked in full view in our driveway. You could see the imprint of where the melting plastic had started. Surprisingly, the inside of the car looked untouched because the windows had been rolled up.

As I turned the key to open the front door, I was not prepared for what I was about to see. I was stunned. Black soot had completely covered all the walls and ceilings, as well as every other surface in our home. My home now felt and looked like something from a horror movie—completely lifeless.

Within minutes, the insurance man appeared, and feeling shaken from what I had just seen, I was not in a good state for a ton of questions.

"Do you mind if I record," he asked, and proceeded to without waiting for a response. Fairly quickly, I felt overwhelmed, like I was under interrogation in a police station. My emotions uncontrollably flooded out of me, and I started crying inconsolably. I was still in a state of shock with it all and was just getting through one moment at a time.

Luckily, the adjustor shared with us that we would be quickly provided with money for food, accommodations, and new clothes. Steve and I left feeling totally depleted, realizing just how much we would be dealing with.

We reached out to close friends, and luckily, they had an extra room where Austin could sleep and Coco would be welcomed while I frantically searched for a furnished home rental.

First of all, I needed to buy us some clothes and basic essentials. So, off to Walmart I went, figuring I could get everything here. I found I was having a hard time focusing on what I needed to buy, still coming to terms with all that just had happened, thinking how on earth was I going to be able to deal with this sense of homelessness and displacement for us all?

Steve and I would be calling the Holiday Inn our home for the next several weeks. After a few nights of this living arrangement, we discovered how differently we dealt with this kind of stress, as our relationship had never been tested in this way before.

We hired Winmar, a restoration company, and Steve and I met them the following Monday to assess the damage and what needed to be done. To my disbelief, just about everything had to be thrown away because of the smoke damage. The whole inside of my home, right down to the studs, was coming out, leaving only a shell of what used to be. As I absorbed this news, I felt sick to my stomach and a huge sense of loss. It wasn't so much the furnishings and material items, as they could be replaced, but it was the cherished items that meant so much—like my son's baby keepsakes, drawings from his childhood, and the books my sister had given me before she passed.

Finally, after three long weeks of being apart as a family, I found a furnished home, luckily close to Austin's high school, where he would soon be starting a new school year. It's a strange feeling, trying to settle into someone else's space. You feel like an unwelcomed intruder that plans on staying way too long. With nothing of my own to bring to warm it up, I felt that I never got totally comfortable living there. However, at least, we were able to be together.

It would take almost a month for them to document every item in our home, even down to the number of paperclips, all of which would be discarded. If there was a bright side to this, at least, we didn't have to prove what we had. Had the fire made its way through the home, destroying everything, there would have been the added stress of proving what we had lost. I was grateful that I didn't have to watch my possessions that meant so much being tossed in a garbage bag. Thankfully, a few things were salvageable, including my treasured Christmas ornaments that had been carefully tucked away in sealed containers and photos, which had been removed from my albums and piled in stacks for me to keep.

After the cleanup, the real work began, as I had to start picking out everything from floors to furniture to handles on kitchen cupboards. Under different circumstances, this would have been fun. However, because of all that I was dealing with, I felt overwhelmed and just wanted to get through it. It was another reminder of the terrible tragedy we had just gone through. In selecting our new furnishings, paint colours, and flooring, I chose not to select anything that resembled what we had, as I did not want to be reminded of what we had lost.

Finally, after six months of feeling unsettled, we were back at a very different-looking home, but it felt like a fresh start. This tragedy affected us all in different ways. But one thing we shared was a deeper appreciation for one another. The outcome could have been very different. As the fire was confined to the garage with my car parked inside, had Austin been in the house much longer, he may not have survived. We all learned the insignificance of material things and realized, even more, the importance of the people and pets that we love. These cannot be replaced.

CHAPTER II

Taking My Health for Granted

For me, July 12, 2017, will be forever a reminder of how, in an instant, our life as we know it can change.

San Francisco is one of my favourite places to visit for many reasons. Napa Valley, only an hour away, offers vineyards that produce some of the most amazing wines. You can find almost any type of food you might desire in San Francisco; being a foodie, I take full advantage any time I visit.

I flew out for the celebration of the birthday of my niece Michelle and the birth of her new baby girl and to reconnect with my great nephew and create some cherished memories. I was filled with anticipation.

Michelle had booked three vineyards in Napa Valley to see, which would start on the first day of my arrival. I had visited San Francisco twice before over the past few years and always took home with me very fond memories.

Michelle, her friend, Michelle's six-week-old baby girl, and I arrived at the first vineyard. As we were seated, we were then greeted by a charming, good-looking young man. He would be bringing the different tastes of this vineyard's best wines, along with some delicious appetizers. Taking in this beautiful, sunny day and the view overlooking the picturesque vineyard, I thought, What could be better?

Since Michelle was nursing, she was the designated driver. We were on our way to the next vineyard, when without any warning, out of nowhere, I saw from the corner of my eye, a black car speeding right toward us. I thought, Oh no! We're going to be hit!

The next thing I remember is opening my eyes up to deployed air bags and seeing white dust floating in the air, blended with a trace of smoke. I worried that the car may blow up.

I frantically fumbled for the door handle and stepped out. I cried out instantly, now feeling excruciating pain. As I looked around, I saw Michelle and her friend were also out of the car, and Michelle was frantically trying to open the door to where her daughter was crying in her car seat. Although shaken up, her daughter, thank God, appeared to be fine. Thankfully we were all in one piece. Looking at one another, I knew this would be a memory we would rather not share. My niece, a nurse, could see the pain I was in and told me to sit down and not to move until the ambulance arrived. An eyewitness to the accident had placed the call.

The first words that came out of my mouth were, "I can't go to the hospital. I don't have any medical insurance." Looking back now, I can't believe that my fear of the cost of treatment trumped my own health. In spite of my potential injuries, I was feeling reluctant to go to the hospital, imagining how this could financially ruin me and my husband.

Once paramedics arrived, a brace was quickly put around my neck and on to the stretcher I went. I noticed my right arm felt numb. As the ambulance rushed to the hospital, I felt every bump while lying on the hard, unforgiving stretcher. I thought to myself that this had to be a bad dream. The drive to the hospital seemed endless, but, thankfully, Michelle was also seated in the ambulance, holding my hand. Although I was grateful for Michelle's support, what I really longed for was to be able to see my husband and son.

Upon my arrival at the hospital, I was quickly put on a gurney to be wheeled to an examining room. Once in the room, I was asked if it was okay to cut and remove my sundress, and I agreed. Before I knew it, my new sundress was quickly cut in two, along with my favourite bra. Damn, why couldn't it have been an old one?

Unable to move without feeling extreme pain, I was administered by IV a type of cocktail, something other than what I had thought I'd be having that day. I certainly would have preferred sipping on a nice glass of Chardonnay, but as we all know, life has a way of taking us somewhere else at times.

Finally feeling the effects of the pain medication, I felt like I was floating, looking down at someone else's misfortune. A doctor appeared, along with his sidekick, and told me they would be taking me for a body scan, as well as other tests. I felt totally dependant on these strangers but realized I had no choice but to believe that they could help me. I was clearly feeling vulnerable.

As I waited for test results, I now observed my surroundings. I realized I was in the emergency area of the hospital. In the bed next to me was a young man who was as high as a kite, chattering away to himself. Next thing I knew, I heard a loud thump, and when I looked over, he was lying on the floor, intravenous and all still hooked in his arm. He was having what seemed to be a seizure—and I thought I was having a bad day. As I watched this man being helped back into his bed, I realized that the fluid being pumped into my body needed to be released.

Oh no, I thought, my dignity will be taken to a new low. As the nurse exposed me and placed the bedpan beneath me, she discreetly looked away. However, it took some concentration to just let it flow.

Shortly after, Michelle appeared and shared some good news. Thankfully, her baby girl had no immediate signs of injury. Thank God for well made car seats! When I asked how she was, she replied fine other than some mild pain and bruising. Michelle had recently had a C-section from delivering her daughter, and I can only imagine the pain she was experiencing, but she was not one to complain. After being examined, Michelle's friend discovered she had suffered a mild concussion.

Michelle then asked if I wanted her to call Steve. I said sure, and she made the call for me. Michelle first spoke to Steve for a few minutes and then gently put the phone up to my ear. I wish I could tell you what I said, but I can't remember—probably due to being high as a kite on the pain medication. All I remember is trying to hold it together, so Steve, a worry wart by nature, would not worry too much.

After saying goodbye to Steve, Michelle, a practising nurse and knowing the system, leaned down and whispered in my ear, "If you don't show them you can walk, they won't release you."

Because of the financial implications, I thought, There is no way in hell that I'm spending any more time here than necessary. And, let's face it, I wouldn't be receiving many visitors.

The doctor arrived to reveal the test results, which showed only a bruised rib and no internal injuries. I was banged up and sore, but he assured me, in time, I would heal. Feeling somewhat relieved, I braced myself for what I would need to do next and show the doctor I was capable of walking on my own. With the help of the doctor, I slowly put one foot on the floor to stand up and held my breath while placing the other foot down. I felt like a baby taking her first steps. Yes, I survived the challenge. The pain was somewhat tolerable due to the drugs that had been administered earlier. I was set free, along with a prescription to ease the pain for the remainder of my week's stay. The doctor offered to write a note to the airline for my immediate return home, but I knew I was still much too sore to sit for a six-hour flight.

Michelle's home in San Francisco was a lovely, century-old two-story home. It was set up like a duplex, with a separate unit on the main floor for their au pair. Thankfully, the au pair had plans to go out of town to visit her boyfriend over the next few weeks and graciously offered me the use of her bedroom while she slept on the couch for a few nights until her departure.

I quickly became aware that my road to recovery was not going to be an easy one. Just getting in and out of bed brought tears to my eyes, the pain at times feeling unbearable. I had never felt so helpless in my life. Because I was staying in the lower-level quarters, there was no other option but to go up and down what seemed to be a never-ending staircase to share in meals, much needed hugs from my four-year-old great nephew, and, of course, let's not forget, the California wine. Yeah, I know what you're thinking, "You're not supposed to drink while on medication," but at this point, this would be one of my much-need pleasures throughout my stay.

Unfortunately, I was unable to pick up my great niece but was still able to touch and smell her, bringing feelings of bonding in a different way. This innocent being was pure, unconditional love and, luckily, had been totally oblivious to what she had just been a part of. Due to the medication, I was on, I certainly was feeling more emotional. I couldn't help but feel an overwhelming sadness that Gale never got to experience these moments of being a grandmother. Cancer took her way too soon.

The time came for me to return home. Unfortunately, I no longer had pain medication to help me through the six-hour flight. I wondered, How the hell am I going to do this? Since Michelle had booked my flights there and back, I was unaware that she had thoughtfully assigned a window seat for me on my return flight. As I slowly inched my way to the window seat, I prayed that the two beside me would remain empty to make it easier when I needed to empty my bladder. I know what you're thinking, "Good luck with that!" As the last people boarded, a woman did claim the aisle seat, but the middle remained empty. I chose to explain my situation to this woman, and she graciously agreed to switch seats. Whew! At least one less thing to worry about.

I had left my car at the airport's "park and fly" in Detroit while away. I knew I was unable to drive, but unfortunately, Steve did not have a passport to cross over the border. Thankfully, Austin and his girlfriend, Paige, both of whom had passports, were able to come to my rescue. My tears flooded out as I hugged my son, recognizing how close I came in never experiencing this moment again. Attempting to get into the passenger side of my car and on no pain medication, it felt like I was climbing a mountain. Up until now, Austin hadn't realized the extent of my injuries, and exhausted from the trip, I could no longer mask the pain. Austin, now twenty, had never seen his mother in such a vulnerable state. The pain I was in was evident as I manoeuvred into the car seat. Our roles reversed, as I now needed his help. Although a little shaken up himself from seeing me like this, he remained focused and drove us home.

Sometimes, there is an unspoken awareness that two human beings share when you both realize just how close you came to never seeing one another again. Once home and embracing my husband, I felt overwhelmed with love, relief, and gratitude to be in his arms again.

Over the next several weeks, I learned physical trauma will force you to rest, whether you like it or not—this is part of the body's healing process. Feeling a loss of control, I was forced to take the next several months away from my real estate business to allow for the necessary time to heal. This would be a first for me to experience having no choice but to just rest and recuperate. I would learn a whole new level of patience. Being a bit of a control freak—okay, maybe a big one—I had to come to terms with letting a lot of things go: housework, laundry, cooking, and the need to have things done a certain way. You would think this would be a welcomed break, but unfortunately, it was not, as it drove me crazy not to be able to do the things I once could do.

In the first two months of the healing process, slow and steady, like the turtle, would be my speed of my life now. I started with massage therapy to help relieve the tightness from whiplash and other muscles. Not quite the enjoyable experience I once remembered—however, it was necessary. I looked forward to the day I would get back to the familiar, more enjoyable, relaxing feeling getting a massage once had.

Fortunately, Michelle had good coverage with insurance on her car. This would provide financial relief of up to 25,000 dollars. At the time, this seemed like it would be a sufficient amount of money toward my treatments needed for recovery. Unfortunately, after seven weeks of using these funds, I received a call from the insurance adjustor explaining that any amount of money that was left on this policy would now go toward the outrageous hospital bill of 75,000 dollars. More time to fully recover was no longer an option financially. Ready or not, back to my business it was.

Meanwhile, back in California, the results of the investigation were now finished and showed that the man who hit us did, indeed, go through a yield sign, and it was determined he was at fault.

Sometimes in life, when we feel we can no longer handle any more, we are tested further. I wish I could tell you why, but I'm still trying to figure this out. Maybe it is to make sure we take nothing for granted. Or maybe it is a reminder to us all that life is full of detours and that we are stronger than we think. Now juggling my business as well as various treatments that I needed in order to heal, I was now also bombarded with emails and phone calls from this man's insurance company asking me to settle. I didn't understand why at first. Eventually, they told me that until I agreed to their low-ball settlement, I would not get a dime for help with the already overwhelming treatment expenses or money lost due to time away from my business. I felt overwhelmed with the constant calls pressuring me to settle and, on one occasion, gave the adjustor a piece of my mind and hung up. These ongoing, pestering calls would not stop. I thought how disgraceful that these insurance companies try to force people back to work before they are able, preying on the vulnerable and hoping they have limited funds and have no choice but to settle quickly. Insurance companies, I think, prey on people's desperation and fragile states of mind.

Fortunately for me, I, at least, had a husband with a job that could support us through this, although barely. The hospital where I had received treatment was also calling constantly, asking for the amount of $64,000, which was still owing. When they first called to inform me of this amount still owing and to ask when I would be paying it, I told them I thought they had the wrong person. I asked how I could possibly owe that much for two-and-a-half-hour visit. They then assured me they didn't have the wrong person and asked how I was going to pay. Owing this amount of money added more stress. I felt even worse, thinking that this could have been avoided had I only taken out travel insurance.

I reached out to Michelle, letting her know about this conversation between me and the hospital. I was in total shock that they could charge this much for such little time. She informed me this is what hospitals do in the States: inflate costs, especially when they're aware that it is an accident and insurance companies are involved.

What a scam, I thought. I certainly had a new appreciation for our health insurance coverage in Canada.

Finally, after two months of weekly massage therapy to relieve the tightness in the traumatized muscles, I was able to start physiotherapy sessions. Having never needed physiotherapy, I did not know what to expect. Well, let's just say, I stuck out like a sore thumb. On my first appointment, I walked into the office of my therapist, Jen, ever so confidently, dressed up in my business attire and high heels, feeling certain I would only need a short time of treatment—here's me wanting to be in control again.

After her assessment and many questions, she said, "You talk a good talk," and informed me that, in my current condition, I would need treatment for at least a year if not longer. I found it interesting that Jen could see just by the way I stood how much my body was out of alignment. (Again, note to self: no matter how much you may want to be in control over certain situations, sometimes we need to learn when to let go.)

At the end of August, for financial reasons, I decided I had to return to my real estate business. I thankfully heard from many clients over the following six months, which transformed into selling many homes and fortunately, became the best six months I had ever experienced in my thirty-plus-year career. I believe my guardian angel, my sister Gale, was watching over me.

After a year of physio, the physiotherapist and I concluded that now at eighty percent recovery, this was probably as good as it was going to get. I welcomed the one less weekly appointment. I continued, however, with monthly massage therapy and chiropractic treatments, now, finally, seeing a light at the end of the tunnel.

However, the following spring, my accident injuries felt the need to revisit me. It started off slowly, like a toothache, and I chose to simply block out the pain, as mentally, I felt unable to face what was really happening. Prior to the accident, 1 was blessed with good health and high energy. I obviously was in denial.

I would say to myself, Look, you've already dealt with all of this. This isn't a good time. I was enjoying my life, feeling I was finally back in control. But soon, I sank into a depression, barely able to get through the day. With the lack of energy, concentration, and in physical pain most days, I finally came to the realization that I needed help and reached out for a doctor's appointment. After explaining to the doctor the pain I was experiencing most days, she examined me and then asked if I was depressed. I wanted to yell, "Hell yes," and told her I was. Even though I know that mental illness is a possibility for many of us, at some point in our lives, I felt the need to justify to her and myself that it was solely because of my physical pain.

As much as I hated to admit it, I learned I still had stigma attached to depression and looked upon myself as being weak. Even after all the years of witnessing my sister Gale dance with her demons and understanding it is a chemical imbalance, I was surprised that I felt I was above this and realized to accept this disease and remove judgement for all, including myself my, I needed to explore more inwardly. I guess, sometimes, even when we think we "got it," we may not have it until we wear those shoes. I was given a prescription for Duloxetine, and then before leaving the office, I was asked ever so nicely to fill out a questionnaire on just how depressed I was. I was mortified, as now I had to put on paper all that I was feeling. In this instant, I knew I was no longer the stable and in-control woman I once was. This was a very humbling experience, to say the least.

Duloxetine, which I Googled as soon as I got home, I learned is a medication used to treat major depressive disorders, anxiety, fibromyalgia, and neuropathic pain. Miss Independence would now take on her new role of "a person in need of help." I had to come to terms and realize what a toll this life's "bump in the road" had taken on me, as well as my husband and my son, especially through these past few months. I can't imagine how helpless they both felt watching me fall apart, once again having no control.

My son, at this time a young man of twenty-three, offered me help. Through his own research, he came to learn that CBD oil has shown to help reduce inflammation and ease pain of all sorts. He surprised me and gave me CBD to try as one of my Christmas gifts. I know I never thought at fifty-eight years old, I'd experience this kind of loving gesture from my son, but I was so grateful that it did bring some relief.

There comes a time in your relationship with your child that a shift occurs. For different reasons, you witness this human that you brought into this world show you compassion and unconditional love on a whole different level. Without being asked, they show up for you and do whatever they can to help. What a gift this is as a parent, to feel this pure unconditional love. Steve, as well, has been my rock and has shown me the patience of a saint. I felt bad as, financially, I knew my time away from work was putting us in debt. Now, with over two years of dealing with constant stress, I was also feeling guilty that Steve had to endure this. I am so appreciative to have these men love me unconditionally through this journey, both here to support me and do whatever they can to help.

This experience has taught me that allowing vulnerability to show up will not always mean pain is to follow. In the company of the right people, it can be a gift. Notice how I said in the presence of the right people. I learned from a young age that I could only rely on myself and was proud of never relying on or needing anybody else.

After being on Duloxetine for three weeks, unfortunately, the pain was only getting worse. With just a few weeks until Christmas, I was becoming desperate for relief. I loved Christmas and wanted to enjoy it as pain free as possible. I was back at the doctor's again when the pain became unbearable. The doctor examined me and said I had tennis elbow. Her, seeing the pain I was in, prescribed a medication, which, thankfully, provided some relief over the Christmas holidays.

Happy New Year! Unfortunately, the pain had returned as a result of being out of medication. The doctor referred me to an orthopedic professional, and after a month of waiting, I received a cortisone shot just in the nick of time. Although the needle was painful, some instant pain relief followed. I did realize this was not a cure but was hopeful that it would help keep the inflammation down while I continued physio.

Finally, I felt like my old self again and was back in my groove, so to speak. Unfortunately, this changed two weeks later, as pain resumed in my neck and right arm. In the meantime, I was scheduled to see the doctor to go over the results of my MRI on my neck, which had been finally ordered after two years. Days before my appointment, I received a call from the doctor's office asking me to come in earlier than scheduled. When I asked why, I was simply told to stop physio treatments. Obviously, I was feeling a little concerned, wondering what the results showed but never anticipated the results I was about to hear.

As I waited in the exam room for the doctor to arrive, I hoped to finally have some answers as to why this pain was continuing and what exactly was causing it. As the doctor shared the results, I felt as if I could see her lips moving but suddenly everything stood still. She disclosed that due to the car accident, I had compression of my cervical spinal cord, with two discs bent halfway into my spine and two others completing crushed. I would require surgery as soon as possible. She would send a referral letter to the Spine Centre in London, Ontario, as we had no neurologist here in Sarnia. Tears came flooding down my face, so she came over and held my hand. I asked how long the recovery would be following the operation, and she replied a year to eighteen months. I think I cried out of relief, finally knowing after two and a half years what was causing my pain and fear of what was to come. Looking at the doctor's face, I wondered if she felt bad for not ordering this MRI earlier. She also shared information that if I lost my bladder control or woke up with numbness in my legs and could no longer walk, I should immediately go to Emergency. This only created more fear as I left her office and was in a state of disbelief and shock. Now for the waiting.

In the meantime, I had another meeting with my lawyer, who I had hired a year ago to represent me in my lawsuit against the man that ran into us with his car. I learned that in California, you have up to two years to file a claim. Although his main practice was Family Law, my lawyer came recommended, so I trusted him. After all, he was a lawyer. In his office, I was ready to tell him about my results of needing spinal surgery. Before I could even speak, he informed me that my case was getting too big for him to handle and he was busy. Okay, didn't see this coming. He said that he had already talked to another local lawyer on my behalf that specialized in accident claims and that she agreed to help me.

I waited to hear from her, and after several weeks of not hearing anything, I decided to contact her. She informed me she was still waiting for my case file. So, I called my previous lawyer's office and was assured it would be sent. Once this new lawyer finally got my file and looked through it all, she contacted me. I would learn that, unfortunately, my previous lawyer had waited until the last day to file my case, exactly the two- year mark, and filed it in the wrong jurisdiction. Instead of filing my case in the state of California, where it happened, he filed it here in Ontario, Canada. I was no longer able to sue the insurance company of the man that had hit me. Feeling once again out of control, I completely broke down, balling. In consulting with a lawyer friend, he advised me that my best course of action would be to sue my previous lawyer for misrepresentation. Having to deal with this now, on top of my surgery, felt overwhelming. I wondered, How am I ever going to get through this?

Two weeks later, I received a letter from the Spine Centre stating that, due to the number of patients, the wait time even before a consultation would be at least eighteen months to two years. I felt, yet again, helplessness and loss of control. Now what?

Having a nurse in the family, definitely, came in handy. I reached out to Michelle and let her know what was going on. She quickly did some research and found a neurologist just over three hours away in Niagara Falls, New York. Since he was outside of Canada, this would not be covered through our health-care system. The cost for this constellation would be 650 dollars, but I felt, at this time, that I had no other option and wanted a professional's opinion. After all, we're talking major surgery here. I called and got an appointment in less than ten days. On our way there, I was feeling anxious that I would find out for sure whether surgery was needed or not.

His office was in what appeared to be in a strip plaza, where other businesses also leased space. As we walked into the sterile, spacious waiting room, I saw where to register and did so. We took a seat, and after what seemed like eternity, the neurologist, well-groomed and not much taller than me, introduced himself and escorted us to his office. He first examined me and then started explaining what he concluded from the viewing of my MRI. I asked if Steve and I could look at the MRI, as I had not seen it yet. Also, I told him it would be easier for me to understand if I could see what he was talking about. As he showed us where the two discs were pressed into my spine on the X-ray, as well as the two discs that were damaged and would need to be replaced, I could feel my eyes start to tear up. I think I needed to see for myself to process my injuries and come to terms with the reality I was facing. I managed to keep it together while the neurologist finished talking and made his recommendation of getting the surgery done sooner rather than later. We thanked him, and he handed us a folder with all the information I would need should I decide to go ahead with the surgery, which, by the way, could be done in eight weeks in the United States at a price of 33,000 American dollars. My steps quickened as I walked toward the exit door. As soon as I was out of the building, my husband reached for me and held me tightly as I uncontrollably balled.

Once home, I was feeling helpless and overwhelmed, partly to do with not having the money available to get the surgery done and also the fear that overtook me. Realizing the urgency of needing this surgery, I reached out to a doctor, who was thankfully one of my friends, and asked for any advice or help she could give. After I explained my situation, she reviewed my MRI and made a referral on my behalf to a neurologist in London, Ontario.

Within days after the referral was sent, I received a call and an appointment was scheduled the following week. I am reminded, once again in life, it is who you know that can make all the difference. I was grateful. In the meantime, COVID-19 was making its destructive debut throughout the world, already taking thousands of lives and spiralling out of control. We were now globally facing a pandemic.

As we drove down this familiar highway, on our way to see another neurologist, it was eerily sparse, with only the odd vehicle. An hour later, we arrived in the city of London, normally filled with the hustle and bustle of traffic, but not that day; it looked lifeless, with very few people out and about.

Upon entering the hospital, we were immediately greeted by staff wearing masks and gowns, asking us to sanitize our hands. It felt and looked like something out of a science fiction movie. We had no idea this would be our new "normal" for quite some time.

Walking down the hall to the right, we were greeted by a lady who escorted us to a small examining room. As my husband and I waited for the neurologist, I felt more at ease this time, probably due to the fact that we were in our own country and closer to home. As well, I knew we would not be faced with a huge medical bill, as, in Canada, we are all covered by our governmental health care

Dr. Sam was a tall, medium-built man, with an aura of calmness about him. He came in, sat down, and introduced himself. Sitting across from us on a stool, he asked what brought us here. I explained my journey, up to this point, as well as my frustration with our medical system. Much to my surprise, he turned out to be on the board of spinal surgeons in London, Ontario. I could tell by the expression on his face, he disliked my opinion about our health-care system. (Note to self, sometimes honesty is not the best policy.) He pulled up my MRI on the screen so that we were all able to see it as he explained what he saw. He also discussed the surgery procedure, along with the risks involved. These risks, shockingly, had been left out by the other neurosurgeon we had seen in the United States.

I had no idea that the surgery performed would go through the front of my neck, close to my larynx, with a small possibility of changing the way my voice sounded or losing it completely. Dr. Sam explained it would eventually relieve any numbness in my arms and legs, along with the extreme pain I constantly felt up and down my right arm. However, some pain would probably still exist in my neck from the whiplash I had sustained. I thought to myself, I guess it was unrealistic to expect that all the pain would be gone after surgery, and I would welcome any relief I could get at this point. I knew I could no longer go on living like this. He showed Steve and me what the imitation discs looked like and explained the goal was that these were to fuse to the spine. He assured me that there was a high success rate with this procedure. He then asked if I was ready to make this decision now or if I needed more time. I broke down crying. Living in pain all the time had taken a toll on me, not just my physical ability but mentally. I looked at my husband, and he knew my decision had been made. I signed the necessary paperwork and was now on the emergency surgery list. I had cried more in these past few months than in my whole life. Understanding we were now in a pandemic, I then asked how long he thought I would have to wait before surgery. He replied, "I honestly have no idea."

Once back home, it seemed like no matter what TV channel I switched to someone was talking about this unknown virus. This now was on everyone's radar; all of us having to grasp that we were now in a pandemic. I think at first, like most of us, I was in a state of shock, never thinking this would be something I would ever experience in my lifetime.

Just about everyone was now being told to "self-isolate" as much as possible. Most businesses, services, and elective surgeries were shut down. It felt like our whole world was coming to a halt. A strong sense of how much we needed each other to cope with this unprecedented situation was being felt worldwide—from medical staff helping to save lives to everyday people helping at grocery stores and other necessary services that were still needed. We were all having to rely on each more than ever.

So, what did this mean for me getting my surgery? I waited helplessly for the phone call and green light to be given. Having this condition now for over two and half years, I felt numbness starting to creep into other areas of my body. Although I was never overly religious, I started praying now more than ever. My left leg and foot were now wobbly when walking, and this only added to my fear. Without surgery soon, I knew that paralysis was a strong possibility. To worry about this, along with the pandemic, was overwhelming, to say the least, but I just tried to take one day at a time. My husband was being extra careful, distancing and sanitizing, constantly as he was still working. He knew the worst thing that could happen right now was for any of us to get this virus, as that would jeopardize my surgery.

Another month passed by, and I was still waiting. I had had several calls over the past few weeks from my neurosurgeon's assistant, Diane. A warm-sounding, upbeat woman, she let me know that as soon as things opened up, I would be one of the first patients in. I was feeling hopeful that it could happen soon, so I thought, I better get myself mentally prepared. Understanding, I had to totally let go of the need for control, I started focusing my mind to fully accept and embrace my situation, preparing as best I could for the journey that lay ahead. Because of this pandemic, did I mention I would be doing this solo, as no visitors were allowed in the hospital? Yikes!

Finally, on May 28, I received the call I was waiting for. In two days, I would be getting my surgery. I was glad the notice was short as I wanted to just get it done!

Steve drove the hour-long drive to the hospital, while I was in the passenger seat, texting Austin letting him know I loved him and would see him in a few days. Steve and I were both in our own thoughts and held hands part of the way. I felt his love and strength and let this flow into me. As we pulled up in front of the hospital, it had started slightly raining. I got out of the car and felt anxiety kick in. I was short spoken with Steve, but he let it go, understanding why. I was reminded how lucky we both were, loving each other enough to just be able to be real with our feelings, imperfections and all. Outside the entrance, we said our goodbye and hugged tightly before I headed in and up the escalator. I never looked back in his direction. I knew it was best not to. I checked in and, while in the waiting area, noticed how few people were there. As I sat with my overnight bag on the floor by my side, looking for distractions on my phone, time now became my focus. The clock showed it was now just a little after nine.

Before too long, a staff member got me and, without wasting any time, directed me along. While undressing and putting my hospital gown on, I was in my head repeatedly saying, Remember, you got this! My total focus now was to get through this and come out in better health. For me, there was just no other option. I still had so much more I wanted to do before leaving this world. I feel our lives are made up of so many different experiences, good and bad, and these challenge us to grow. It is our choice how we respond to them, and perspective is everything!

Change, as we know, is inevitable. As I've gotten older, I've learned it's better to go with the flow. Throughout the falls I've had in my life, there were times I just wanted to give up, but as we all know, you need to get back up, realizing there are no guarantees but hope that things will get better. I have not met, so far in my fifty-eight years of living, anyone who has reached these moments of total bliss without experiencing adversity or heartache. I think this is what is needed in order to feel the real, magical moments of life. When life is in that sweet spot, it helps us forget all the pain, whether mental or physical, that was needed to go through in order to get us there. My choice in life has always been to keep on trying. I would rather risk the chance of failing again and again than to take no chance at all. After all, without hope, what is left?

Finally, in the preoperative area, where I was hooked up to intravenous, I waited in a bed. The time now 9:30 a.m. I settled in as I knew it would be hours still before surgery. In the meantime, I scanned around the room, focusing on a man across from me lying in his bed. I'm guessing he was in his late fifties, and he was filling his time by talking on his phone. I wondered what he was getting done. With my overnight bag sitting on a chair beside my bed, I got my phone out, too. I had no desire to talk to anyone, as my goodbyes were already said. My focus was to remain in a calm, mental state.

The time now 12:30 and anxiety was just starting to break through my calm state. Thankfully, the surgeon was ready for me, and just like I'd seen in the movies, I was wheeled down to "where it all happens."

Well, I thought, no turning back now. I felt grateful that I was getting my surgery done, as I was well aware of how many others were still waiting. As I was wheeled into a big, sterile-looking room, I saw two men and two women suited up and ready to get things started. On one side, I had the anesthesiologist, ready with face mask in hand, and on the other side, a nurse. When the nurse looked into my eyes, she could see my fear. She gently touched my shoulder, saying, "Everything will be fine." It was exactly what I needed to hear at that moment. I was so appreciative of her kind words.

As I came to after the six-hour surgery, till foggy, I could hear a woman continually screaming out a name. At first, I thought I was dreaming. After a few minutes, I then realized, listening to her, that she was calling out for her dog. It reminded me of my mother-in law, who has dementia; it was all too familiar and I started crying. When a nurse came in minutes later, I asked if I could be moved. I didn't have the strength to deal with the screaming woman at that moment, especially while trying to heal. With an annoyed look on her face, she left to see what she could do. As luck would have it, another nurse in the room, overheard our conversation. She then came to my bed, leaning close to me, and whispered that she totally understood, as she, too, had a mother with this terrible disease. Thankfully, she moved me to another room. My new roomie was Jack, a quiet, elderly man, and I was relieved.

I looked down at my hands, seeing a needle in each one. I also had a drainage tube coming from my neck. I was so relieved the surgery was over, other than feeling like a Mack truck had hit me. As I looked at my surroundings, I noticed a basic round clock that hung in the middle of the wall, straight ahead of me. I could see the time was now 6:30 p.m. The nurse arrived to check on me and showed me how to work the morphine pump. She told me I could push the button whenever I needed pain relief. For the next, twenty-four hours, this would be my best friend.

Not having eaten all day, I was starving. I had missed the dinner hour, so she offered a choice between two sandwiches, and tuna it was. I quickly learned moving my neck at all was painful. I had two ruffs, which were tube-shaped cotton-filled supports, tied loosely around my neck as a reminder to move with caution. These looked like long sausages. My throat was swollen where they entered through the front of my neck, and while eating this sandwich, I felt like I was trying to swallow glass through a straw, but with help of some juice, I was able to get the sandwich down.

Once I finished eating, it was time to relieve myself. This would be another whole new experience. At this point, I needed help just to get in and out of bed. The nurse told me, as she assisted me to the bathroom, how necessary it was to use a walker for support to ensure that I didn't fall. I thought to myself, "I certainly don't want to undo the painstaking and precise work that the neurosurgeon had provided me."

Not remembering much of the night, other than waking up to push my button for pain relief, the next thing I knew was waking to daylight streaming through our big window. I heard a nurse's voice helping my roommate, Jack, back from the washroom. Listening to his soft voice and good manners, I instantly liked this man. Seeing I was awake, the nurse helped me up to do the same. Now for some breakfast. I had never had an extended stay in hospital before and had no idea what to expect for meals, other than the stories you hear about how bad the food is. It certainly proved to be true, and after eating a oatmeal for breakfast, it would be all downhill from there. For dinner, we were served meatloaf. After a few bites, I instantly became a vegetarian throughout my stay, excluding tuna sandwiches which became my staple.

Later in the day, out of nowhere it seemed, a short, fit man stood at the end of my bed. After introducing himself as a physio therapist, he quickly started eyeballing me for a neck brace, bringing several out and putting them up against my neck for sizing. After he chose one, he explained he would be back tomorrow, and if he felt I was strong enough, he would consent for me to be released. I was beginning to understand the important role this stranger would play for me to go home. So, I wondered what other hurdles would I encounter.

Twenty-four hours after my surgery, I was disconnected from my morphine pump. In replacement, I would be given two doses of pain reliever every four hours. Keeping track of time became my priority, as the stronger medication slowly wore off and I began to experience more pain, which, at times, was intolerable.

On day two after surgery, I was able to get up out of bed on my own and used my walker to get where I wanted to go. It was late morning, and I knew that, at some point that day, I would see the doctor. He would be the one to make the final decision on whether I could be released or not. In the meantime, my "physio guy" showed up and seemed surprised to see me standing with a walker.

"Are you feeling up to taking a walk down the hall?" he asked.

"Okay." I wondered what my task would be.

As we neared the end of the hall, he instructed me to turn right, where I saw a small set of stairs, four going up to a landing and four going back down. Slow and steady, I walked up and down, while holding on to the rails. Mission accomplished!

Back in my room, I was told that an X-ray needed to be taken to assure the doctor that everything was fine. Sitting in a wheelchair, steered by a porter, I was on my way get this done. The hallways seemed eerily empty, except for staff.

After arriving at our destination, sharing some pleasantries, I waited alone in a spacious hallway outside of where the X-ray would be done, not a soul in sight. While I waited, my imagination got the best of me. I started thinking what I would do if some mad man was roaming the hallways, who somehow had made it into the hospital unseen. Okay, maybe a little dramatic, I agree, but I'm blaming this on the drugs.

Returning to my room, there stood a man dressed all in white. I didn't recognize him; however, he was a member of the surgery team. As he was talking, asking how I was, I saw imprinted on his sleeve his name along "Doc." He looked surprised that I was up and about and, due to this, signed my release papers. I made the call to hubby to come and get me.

As I changed into my street clothes, I realized that I would need a top with a large neck opening for my new accessory—my neck brace. For the first time since my surgery, I looked at myself in the mirror and the reflection revealed just how much this surgery had taken out of me. My face was drained of any colour.

Waiting at my room's door for a porter to come and get me, I realized in my rush to leave, I had not said goodbye to Jack. We had been able to hear one another over the past few days, but since a drape was always drawn for our privacy, I had no idea what this man looked like. Before peeking my head around his drape, I called out his name, and for the first time, I saw what he looked like. He was exactly what I imagined: a kind-faced gentleman in his mid-eighties. I wished him well and will never forget what he said to me: "I am an old man with not a lot of time left. You still have many years left, so whatever you do, don't waste any of it!" Jack was a ray of light in this difficult time.

Steve was happy and relieved to see me but, like me, had no idea what to expect next. Upon arriving home, Austin was home to greet me. He, too, like Steve, was glad this was behind us now.

Unfortunately, due to the pandemic, not a lot of preparation was shared prior to my surgery as to what to expect after, other than the healing time of one year to eighteen months. I quickly discovered when I went to lie down on our bed that, due to being weak from surgery and still in a lot of pain, this would not be possible. We realized that I would need a bedrail for support. You can rent these from our local wellness store we discovered. Once set up, I tried again with no success. I quickly discovered how much of your upper body strength is connected to your neck. Feeling more pain because of the exertion, I started crying and asked Steve, "What are we going to do now?"

Desperate for a solution, we were even considering paying thousands of dollars for an adjustable bed. However, we quickly discovered by searching online, that this luxury item came at a much heavier price than anticipated, 7,000 dollars. Okay, now for a Plan B. By sheer luck, we checked with the store where the bedrail came from and they had a solution. They informed us that they had one hospital bed left to rent. We had no idea you could even rent one of these at a cost of only 250 dollars per month. We got the bed delivered and set up downstairs in our rec room, and this enabled me to make adjustments when needing to get in and out of bed.

Thankfully within days, I was strong enough to use the bedrail upstairs on our bed. I missed sleeping in my own bed and the comfort that this brought. I'm sure our neighbours wondered what was going on since this bed had only just been delivered.

During the first few weeks, Austin made me delicious protein fruit smoothies every morning in hopes this would help to heal my body. I felt so grateful to have these men by my side helping me through this difficult time.

One positive thing about the pandemic was that my son was available 24/7 to help me, as he was not working. Steve, an essential worker, took two weeks of vacation to be with me for support and help. Unfortunately, we were not aware that after having this surgery, I needed someone home with me for the first eight weeks while I had to wear the hard neck brace and rebuild my strength. Every time I lay down, I needed someone to remove the brace and put it back on before I got up from the bed.

Before I came home, Steve tried to find a bell that I could ring when I needed help replacing the neck brace each time I got out of bed. With no bells to be found, a bike horn would do to get the attention of the guys when I needed to get up. This was especially important first thing in the morning when time was of the essence to relieve myself. Every time I honked it, it reminded me of a clown horn; I must admit it added a bit of humour to the situation, and I'd call out to whomever was available, "Send in the clown." Humour is a necessity, I believe, to help get you through even the most overwhelming of situations.

I know Steve loves me, but sometimes the man drives me crazy with his over worrying nature, so I welcomed the time when he did go back to work. I was ready for some alone time. Two weeks of both my guys constantly hovering over me was more than enough.

For the next six weeks, Austin would be my primary caregiver. As more time passed, I could tell he was struggling with the pandemic and how it was affecting his mental health. I realized he was not just dealing with the effects of the pandemic, but also having to see his mother in such a vulnerable state. I tried to reassure him that we would be okay, but both of us knew, deep inside, how much this pandemic would affect our way of living. On a positive note, we hadn't spent this kind of time together since he was a child before entering school. We talked a lot, and he made our favourite pancakes. I valued this time together, as I knew another opportunity to spend this kind of time together would probably never happen again. Don't get me wrong, there were definitely days that we needed our own space, but our relationship through this all became closer. As a mother, I never dreamed that there would be a day where I would feel so dependent on my child.

If I only share one thing that I really missed while having to wear my neck brace all the time, it would be a shower and hair wash. I washed my body using a face cloth, but let's face it, that's like putting on your dishwasher for half the time. For my hair, I discovered a cap-like item you could buy for ten bucks. In order for this cap to do its job, it needed to be warmed up in the microwave. Amazing, the stuff you can find on Amazon. Whoever was available would place it on my head, hair totally up inside, and massage gently for two minutes. When we took it off my hair felt and looked like it had just been washed. (Warning to anyone who is going to use this product: after several weeks of usage, you could start losing your hair because the cleaner is quite strong.)

After a month of wearing my neck brace, I was feeling claustrophobic and just wanted to rip it off at times. It was now becoming mentally more challenging. Since this was not an option, I knew I had to keep busy doing something that would take my mind off this. If I was ever needed an excuse to drink more, eat more, or sleep more, this would have been the time. As tempting as this was, I started connecting more on the social media site LinkedIn. I found I liked the platform because I was able to connect with people from all over the world—people that were in business, entrepreneurs, coaches, writers—and this drew me to a new community. I found I enjoyed the connection with other like-minded people that were living their dream life, or at least striving for it. Some I saw were making a difference in a huge way. I guess I liked the whole feel of this community. At a time when I felt so isolated and vulnerable, I welcomed making new friends who had similar interest.

Remember the saying, "Look for the silver lining," I discovered this while going through one of my most challenging adversities. This time would also prove to be another opportunity to improve on my writing skills since this was something that I could still do while healing. I started writing inspirational poetry on LinkedIn and found that some people liked it.

Following one of my posts, a reader reached out and asked me to be a guest speaker on her podcast. I accepted, even though I wasn't quite sure what a podcast was. I thought, Why not? A new adventure. She asked me to talk about this latest chapter of my life's journey, which fit in perfectly with her podcast "Don't Die Before Your Dead." It turned out to be a lot of fun, and I'm so glad I did it!

Now, at a point where I no longer needed to wear a neck brace, I could start physio. This time around, I knew exactly what to wear. Again, I would need months of physio, but this time, it would be different. I felt more confident that my outcome would have long-lasting results. I would work on getting stronger and, once and for all, get past this injury.

The lease on my car was soon coming to an end, and I needed to choose another vehicle. Unfortunately, still not strong enough to drive, I had to choose one without taking a test drive. Austin, like most young men his age, had done a lot of research on cars. He recommended a Subaru Crosstrek. So, we went online, and I picked one in a baby blue colour and ordered it. By the time the car arrived, thankfully, I was strong enough to drive again. Finally, I started to look forward to getting back some independence

Now that I can finally see a light at the end of the tunnel, this is what I learned: We are stronger than we think. Never take life for granted. Don't forget how precious the gift of love is from others. Above all else, in a minute, your life can change as you know it, so live every day to the fullest and embrace all that life offers.

CHAPTER 12

Before the Last Petal Drops

My later-in-life, unexpected gift of receiving a mother-in-law was truly a blessing. Because we lived so far apart, our relationship would not start to develop for several years. On our initial visit, Steve and I stayed at his parents' home in Fort Erie, which is three hours from where we lived. We had been dating for three months and our relationship was getting serious.

Aubrey, Steve's father, and I connected immediately. He had a sense of humour, and there was an instant and easy acceptance of one another. June, Steve's mom, on the other hand, was "lukewarm" and felt distant. From the beginning, she made it quite clear that she had an ongoing, close relationship with her ex-daughter-in-law and it wasn't something she was prepared to give up. Even though Steve and Louise had been apart for thirteen years, their wedding album lay on the coffee table in June's living room. I wondered if this was placed out in full view for me to see. It was certainly hard not to notice. Needless to say, this did not make me feel as welcomed as I had hoped.

On the way home, I was upset and cried; I didn't understand why she felt the need to do this. I thought she would be happy for her son. He had found love again after eighteen years of being on his own. It would take me several years to realize it wasn't me personally, but her fear of losing the close relationship she had with her ex-daughter-in-law.

I found June's relationship with Louise, after all these years, a bit strange, especially when there were no grandchildren. However, after getting to know June, I understood why. In her opinion, just because Steve and Louise's relationship had ended, why should she then be obligated to end her relationship with her daughter-in-law? After all, she had established a close bond over the ten-plus years they were married. The two of them had shared years of shopping together, lunches, and many deep conversations, along with much laughter and tears. Although Steve would have preferred a complete break of all ties with his ex-wife, his mother felt differently. I eventually came to respect June for this.

For the first few years of our marriage, June continually talked about Louise whenever she was with us. It was like an impulsive need, and she couldn't help herself. I came to understand how much she valued this relationship. One day, while Steve was at work, I addressed the "elephant in the room." While June was visiting, helping me wrap presents, I asked her if she could please refrain from bringing up Louise, as it was upsetting Steve. I explained that from Steve's perspective, he had moved on and, all these years later, did not want to be reminded of her and that part of his life. I shared with her how I understood why she held on to this close relationship and let her know that I felt the more people who loved and cared for you, the better. I told her I admired her sense of loyalty and looked forward in creating our own relationship. Even though they remained close, she never brought up Louise again.

Unfortunately, after only a year of being married, Steve's father died. I was grateful of the opportunity and time to get to know him. June, now age seventy-eight, wanted to remain in her home where she had created memories with her husband, even if this meant being alone and three hours away from her only child. Since she came from a generation of women who totally relied on a man to take care of them, I was impressed that, at this stage in her life, she learned how to be independent. Unfortunately, June had given up driving years before, and her husband's car just sat in their driveway for several years after his death. We encouraged her, after a year, to think about selling his car, as it was slowly rusting away. But she was determined that the car would remain where it was, as she hoped to resume driving one day. At least, that was what she told herself. However, we eventually recognized that it was not about the actual car but about what the car represented. The presence of this once well-cared-for car, that now never left the driveway, was a sense of security and memories for June, especially now living alone.

On her own, June came to visit several times a year and stayed long enough to create some beautiful memories. We shared lots of our favourite foods, including pizza, which was something she would never order on her own. At times when I was troubled, she would, in her own calming way, share some of her wisdom and perspective. But only when asked. Her heart-felt wisdom always left me feeling better. I wished that we lived closer. When she wasn't here, we always talked every Sunday morning. Not having had a close relationship with my own mother, I realized all that I had missed out on. Oh, how I miss this now!

We've all heard the saying, "Men marry someone like their mothers," and up until now, I had never given this much thought. I had come to recognize that June and I shared a love for the same foods, styles in clothes, taste in jewelry, movies, and, oh yes, playing the slots. One night, we stayed at a casino until seven a.m.; we had pulled an all-nighter. At eight-two years young, June had as much energy as I did. There were times it was hard to keep up to her. I love that she put no limitations on herself due to her age. In fact, when talking about the next stage of her life, possibly a retirement home, she would say she couldn't envision living with a "bunch of old people." She never saw herself as old, proving to me that your age doesn't have to reflect your state of mind. When I married Steve, I had no idea what a gift his mother would become and the unconditional love we would share.

With time moving forward and months passing between visits, I didn't anticipate what was coming. At Christmas time, Steve would pick June up and bring her to our home to spend the Christmas holidays together. I was so grateful at this special time of the year for us all to be all together. With presents to unwrap and turkey to stuff, let the fun begin. On Christmas morning, I usually woke June with her morning tea. But as I sat with my much-needed morning caffeine, I heard June's bedroom door open. Approaching her to say good morning, I instantly saw the blank look and fear on her face. I stopped dead in my tracks.

"Where am I, and who are you?" she said.

Not knowing what was happening, I reminded her of where she was and who I was. She seemed a bit off balanced, so I escorted her to the couch to sit down. I was now feeling scared, wondering if June had had a stroke. Then, as if it had never happened, she was suddenly back. She blamed the incident on having a bad dream and feeling disoriented. I, on the other hand, sensed it was much more.

As usual, months passed again before we saw her in the spring. When she visited, I would pick out a movie series that I thought we both would enjoy and, of course, a full supply of our favourite treats. We both loved Downton Abbey, and we would sometimes binge watch together, both of us feeling like kids staying up way past their bedtime. Little did I know, at this time, how priceless these memories would become for me. Both Steve and I could tell that her memory was starting to fail her and she was also losing weight–never a good combination when one is living alone. So, with a little coaxing, June agreed to at least start looking at retirement homes in Sarnia, where we lived. We finally found one that called to her, and she went on the waiting list. Now, for the hardest step yet, selling her cherished home that had so much of her life's memories seared into its bones, where she raised her son and shared happy times with her husband.

In a strong seller's market, June's beloved bungalow didn't take long to sell. We were hearing from neighbours and friends about her forgetfulness, and we realized that this was just in time. This, along with the fact that her clothes were now starting to hang off her and groceries were not being eaten, meant it was time for June to be taken care of.

This retirement home was a five-minute drive from our house and was the perfect fit. June approved of its cozy atmosphere and cleanliness. In order to help her settle in, we shared some meals with her over the next few weeks. I have to say the food was actually pretty good. I had the impression that the quality of food would not be very tasty in these places. We made sure her new one-room home was filled with some of her familiar and favourite furnishings, along with a few of her treasured pictures on the walls. I can only imagine how hard it was for June having to let go of so many possessions, but Steve and I were relieved that we would longer have to worry about whether she had taken her medication or eaten. June settled in nicely, and all was well.

As we know, things constantly change in our lives and, unfortunately, sometimes not for the better. We noticed, after six months of her being here, June's memory was getting worse. She would hide things and forget where she put them, especially the key for her door. This was a big sign that there was more happening here than just memory loss.

Once, while visiting, June pointed across the room and proceeded to tell me, "That's my daughter." The lady to whom June pointed was well into her eighties. My heart sank, but after feeling that initial sense of impending loss, I pulled myself together and explained to her that I was her daughter-in-law and that the lady she was pointing at lived here as well. Shortly after this episode, Steve took June to the hospital for a routine, in-and-out procedure. Although she was given no anesthetic, when June tried to get up, she was dizzy and lost her balance. Because she was ninety, the doctor decided to keep her overnight and run some tests. It was no surprise to us to find out that she was in the first stages of dementia. June would require care around the clock. She would not be returning to the home she just settled into.

Neither Steve nor I had any idea of what was going to happen. We were both still working, and with no medical training, it was not possible for June to live with us. Because there were no beds available in our immediate area, June had to remain in the hospital for three weeks until a room finally came up in a nursing home, which, unfortunately, was thirty miles away from us. With only two days' notice, we scrambled to find a mover, resigning ourselves that we had no choice but to move her to the first available nursing home. I can only imagine how she must have felt having to be moved, yet again, into another unfamiliar environment.

Up until now, I had never been in a nursing home and I had no idea what to expect. As the elevator door opened, I instantly smelled an ever-so-slightly foul odour, followed by noises that were completely unfamiliar. Walking down this sterile-looking hall, searching for June's room, I was shocked to see people looking so fragile and depleted, while others wandered aimlessly up and down this hall. The worst, though, was hearing the screaming of a few, which sounded like wounded animals. I was shocked. Surely someone had made a mistake—my mother-in-law doesn't belong here!

Halfway down the hall, I found June sitting by herself in a chair outside her room. She looked like a scared, lost child. Once aware of our presence, June couldn't hold back the tears, asking why she was here. I hugged her. It felt like neither one of us ever wanted to let go. I so badly wanted to take her out of this nightmare, but I knew, unfortunately, this wasn't an option. Steve and I did not have the means financially to afford the kind of care she required at our home. If I ever wished to win a lot of money, it would be now.

The distance and both of us working full time meant weekly visits were all that was manageable. As much as I love this lady, it would take all that I had some days to visit and be reminded of the environment she was living in. This was also a reminder of my own mortality. From what I could see, June was the highest-functioning person at this home, and I so hoped she would be able to find friendship there.

Dementia is such an unforgiving disease, robbing us of what we value the most in our lives: our memories of a lifetime and the connection with our loved ones. June was always so grateful for our visits and, of course, her favourite chocolate bars that we would bring along. I dread the day when she no longer knows who I am.

I think for me, going through this journey at fifty-seven, made me realize even more the importance of time: how valuable it is, how quickly it goes, and not to waste it, which brings to light even more what I still want to accomplish and experience.

Finally, after June was at this home for eighteen months, we would receive a call that a bed finally came available at a nursing home closer to us. I must say, we were oblivious to how our health-care system worked in Ontario and were shocked when given only given twenty-four hours to decide if we even wanted to make this move. Because we were feeling overwhelmed by all of this, we had already talked with someone at the Alzheimer's Society for support and information about how another move might affect June. We were told that her transition should be fairly smooth, and that being able to see us more would be beneficial for us all. With her memory fading, the counsellor suggested that June wouldn't even notice the change. She was right.

As I approached June's new residence to visit her for the first time, I was hopeful that this nursing home would provide a better environment for her final days. In entering this much-older building, I immediately noticed it was in need of some updating. The carpet looked well-worn and there were scuff marks on the walls. This was a reminder of just how many people had once called this their final home. I then reminded myself that you can't judge a book by its cover. On the elevator going up to her floor, I felt like a kid at Christmas and was hoping that this move would prove to be all that we had hoped for.

Stepping out of the elevator, I instantly heard and felt a calmness in the air. In full view was an open-concept, welcoming dining room, along with several other sitting areas. Although it looked outdated, there was a feeling of a familiar place, like when visiting your grandma's home as a child—well-lived in and comfortable. To the right side of this open area, there sat a few overstuffed recliners in a row, with coffee tables in between. And there I found my mother-in-law, with her feet up, sipping on a cup of coffee; she looked like she had been there much longer than a day. My heart was filled with joy seeing her settle in so quickly. The staff here were much friendlier, and there were fewer residents, which meant she would get better care. Steve and I would now be able to visit her more often.

I knew this disease had now taken away her ability to concentrate on reading, so I figured the next best thing would be for me to read to her. Whenever I do, I feel her love while I hold her hand, sitting next to her. This has become our special time and is a ritual at every visit. I am so happy that she will be spending her final days in a more relaxing and caring environment. I'm not sure when the day will come when she no longer recognizes me, but until that day, and even after, I will make sure she feels my unconditional love for her as she has given me all these years.

Just like that, it seemed, the time had come. June no longer recognized who I was. Like fresh snow falling on the ground, only to vanish from the warmth of the sun. I desperately looked for signs of recognition, hoping somehow our close bond would resurface. You spend your life creating memories that this disease, dementia, just slowly takes away. With my tears are mixed emotions, but I believe there will come a day when we'll again be able to recall our memories and those feelings attached.

I wrote this chapter in honour of the special relationship I share with my mother-in-law, June, who showed me unconditional love in such a beautiful, unexpected way.

CHAPTER 13

Thank God for Friends

Friends are undeniably precious souls we meet along life's journey. Some stay longer, while others are here only for a pit stop.

Patricia

My first friend I can remember was Patricia. We met at school in Grade 1 and lived in the same neighbourhood. She was taller and slender with sandy-brown hair. I loved going over to her home for a playdate, as it was a break from my very different home environment. Our favourite spot was in her unfinished basement under cobwebbed stairs. We made our own special space there with our favourite dolls and blankets. We would laugh together and play for hours, oblivious to the outside world.

In the summertime, an above-ground pool would be set up in her backyard, and, boy, did we have fun swimming and playing for hours. At her house, I would get my taste for scary movies while we watched the Saturday afternoon matinee Sir Graves Ghastly on her television. I loved how before the movie would start, the host, looking like Dracula, would rise halfway up out of his coffin and do the introduction of the movie matinee that would be featured. Eating popcorn throughout the movie while getting scared began my passion for scary movies. Our time together ended when I was nine, as this was when my mother left my father and moved me and my siblings to another city. Saying goodbye to my first best friend was gut wrenching, and we both cried while hugging each other on the playground. It was in that moment and time that I realized just how much I would miss my dear friend.

Debbie

While living in Chatham from age nine to eleven, I made friends with a girl my age that happened to live across the street from me, "another Debbie." Although I lived in a home that had four separate units, her home was just for her family. We hung out, it seemed, mostly outside during nice weather, riding our bikes and talking about girl stuff, especially as we were starting to notice boys. Debbie's older brother was away in the army, and I'll never forget the day her family was notified that her brother had died. Understandably, she was very upset. This was the first time I had ever experienced seeing someone that I cared for go through such a loss. I felt scared and sad for her. I did not know how to comfort her, other than just being there. Unfortunately, after only eighteen months, my mother moved us again.

Donna

In Hamilton, Ontario, I was introduced to Donna, a curly redhead that would teach me lessons that I would not soon forget.

Another new school, and I was now going into Grade 6. The school was not in the most desirable of area and on the wrong side of the tracks, so to speak. What I did notice right away was a bakery right across the street, where everyday, we got to smell homemade bread and doughnuts. I sometimes would dream of donuts and in my dream could pick out any and all that I wanted!

I can't remember the exact moment we became friends, but what I can tell you is I'm glad we did. She was feisty and well seasoned, living in one of Hamilton's roughest neighbourhoods. I, on the other hand, looked like Bambi without a clue. I quickly learned how to act tough, because if you showed any fear, you would be picked on. Having a tough girl as a friend helped keep the bullies at bay.

I remember the first time Donna invited me over to her home. What I saw surprised even me. This run-down-looking house from the outside just got worse when I entered. It was filthy and smelled of cigarettes and alcohol. The floors were well worn and the colour of the paint on the walls no longer noticeable, due to the yellow stains from smoke.

Her mother, with the same red curly hair and barely five feet tall, who was recently remarried for the third time, was sitting in the kitchen. When introduced, I could see the hardened lines of life etched in her face; she looked worn out and tough as nails. Her husband didn't look much better. Between the two of them, they blended six children together, and it was evident from what I saw that the two youngest of the six were treated the worst. They were constantly teased, and I couldn't help but feel sorry for them. I sensed after visiting several times that there was much more going on in this home than met the eye—a worse environment than even I was living in.

Donna introduced me to cigarettes and tough boys with an attitude. Unfortunately, I liked both. With not much time allowed out on my own, I would enter quickly in and out of this hopeless world of survival with quick pleasures. Seeing dysfunction on this level was not all that uncomfortable, as I already lived in a relatable world myself. However, it did teach me that there are always people in worse situations than you.

Kate

At twelve years old, I was now living with my father, his wife, and her children. Although we still lived in Hamilton, my father and his new family lived in a more affluent area. Attending yet another new school, I met Kate. She was shorter than me, and at only five feet two inches had an attitude of pushing life to the limits. She was cute with wavy brown hair, freckles, and a lot of personality. I was attracted to her self-confidence and no-fear attitude, pushing the envelope, regardless who was watching. Although I thought our friendship would last forever, Kate taught me that people can grow apart. As difficult as it was, I ended our friendship later in our adult years after realizing that we no longer shared the same values.

Lois

I met Lois when I was seventeen. She was a hostess where I got hired and she trained me. We instantly hit it off. With her blonde hair and striking green eyes, she was beautiful. I loved her laughter and her disposition. I was in awe.

She was married and four years older than me. A mother already to a beautiful son and seemed to have it all. But as we all know, looks can

131

be deceiving, and her marriage dissolved not long after we met. She taught me how a woman could successfully pick up the pieces and move forward with her life, even though her future now looked very different and uncertain. We would occasionally go out on a weekend night to discos, which back then was the new craze, and danced the night away. Two blondes together, we turned a few heads and were bought drinks throughout the night, which, by the way, we both appreciated, as money was tight.

Within a few years, though, Lois would remarry and, unfortunately, move away due to her husband's work. We've always stayed in touch, and no matter the distance or place we are in our lives or the number of years that have gone by, when we do reconnect, it has always been as if I just saw her yesterday. This dear friend, my longest to date, has taught me the value of having a friendship last no matter what's going on in each other's lives—such a treasure. It has been years since I last saw Lois, but I know when we do get together, we will pick up right where we left off.

Cheryl #1

I was almost ready to give birth to my first child when I received a call from Cheryl's husband, Mario. He was inquiring about selling a rental home they owned.

They had recently had their first child, a daughter. After meeting Cheryl and seeing her joy of motherhood, my fears were lessened of becoming a mother myself. She shared honestly about the changes that were ahead for me, along with the overwhelming feeling of love she felt for her daughter. This created an instant bond between the two of us.

Our friendship, now reaching the twenty-five-year mark, has lasted through raising our children together, the loss of parents, and our own personal growth, all the while creating beautiful, laughable, loving moments. With a heart so full of kindness and compassion, it's not hard to understand why I love her so.

Cheryl #2

As fate would have it, our children, would become best friends. Austin started Grade 1 in a new French emersion school and became fast friends with identical triplets. Although looking the same, they very much had their own personalities, and Austin connected easily to all three. Whenever Austin asked for them to come over, I never hesitated, as they were all friends and I didn't want any of them feeling left out—so let the party begin! I quickly realized how much energy it took to have all four of them together and developed an instant respect for their mother, Cheryl, who also had three other children at home! We got to know each other through volunteering at their school and then easily transitioned to setting up playdates together, which also included the two of us.

With our children in some of the same activities, we would watch them and then took turns going back to one another's home. The children played while we indulged in adult conversation and a glass or two of wine. We lived in walking distance of each other, so this made it even more handy.

Another blessed friendship that I still have to this day, I have had the fortune to grow with this woman while watching her conquer so much in her life. We've cheered each other on while wishing the best for one another and cried together through life's adversities and losses. Her ability for patience and unwavering love for those to whom she is connected make her truly a priceless gift to all!

Cheryl #3

(Yes, as fate would have it, three of my besties all have the same name.) With long legs that would stop a bus, Cheryl stands well above my five-foot-three frame. Her down-to-earth nature made it easy for me to become friends with her. I met Cheryl as she was working as a cashier at my local grocery store. We discovered that we both had lost sisters to cancer and shared similar outlooks in life. Although very different in our upbringing—she was a farm girl and me a city girl—our friendship has taught me over the years to have more patience and also the importance of respecting one another's differences.

Audrey

Fate has a funny way of connecting us sometimes. While dealing with the news of Austin's father having pancreatic cancer, I reached out to Audrey, a therapist whose specialty was bereavement. Within that one-hour therapy session, we discovered some similarities, and Audrey explained that the process of journaling would help me "go to the pain to get through it." Although difficult at times, she was absolutely right.

Little did I know, years later, we would reconnect through Facebook. I shared with Audrey, also a local author, the beginnings of an idea that would turn my journaling into a book.

Audrey's belief in my ability to express through writing has been an unexpected gift, and I will always be grateful for her encouragement and support throughout writing my book.

In conclusion, because I did not have the support and love I needed from my parents as I was growing up, my friends became even more of an essential lifeline to my well-being. I have been blessed over the years with friends that have become an extension of my family, loving and supporting me through my life, teaching me lessons, being there when I felt so very much alone and able, above all else, to love me unconditionally. Friends, to me, are such an important part of our lives, and I couldn't imagine my life without them.

EPILOGUE

Little did I know, at age fifty, that my new practice of journaling would take on legs of its own. In writing, I discovered how therapeutic it was to express and release my feelings. I recognized the more I wrote, the more I was ready to uncover all the pain and dysfunction that I had experienced throughout my life and had stuffed down. I began to understand the healing that needed to take place in order for me to live my life no longer imprisoned by the demons of past generations. I now had the time and strength to dig deeper and look at things that had been too painful to deal with before. I discovered the power of writing and how it could help me put things in perspective and see things more clearly.

I decided to share some of my life's experiences and lessons in hopes of helping others realize they are not alone. We all need to be seen as human beings, deserving the help that we need to heal and to live our best lives while we are here. When we start being compassionate with ourselves, we can, then, begin the healing process. Confronting the truth and feeling the pain allows us to move on to freer living. We are not defined by circumstances over which we have no control.

My hope is that the stigma that is still so extremely attached to dysfunction can be uncovered without guilt, shame, or judgement. That, as a society, we can learn to come together and help one another more, recognizing the importance of breaking this unforgiving cycle. We all deserve to feel connected, loved, and appreciated for all that we are. Life, my friend, is too short to live any other way.

CPSIA information can be obtained
at www.ICGtesting.com
Printed in the USA
BVHW031611190322
631809BV00007B/63